The Conferring Church

The Conferring Church

By

M. Richard Troeh and Marjorie Troeh

The Reorganized Church of Jesus Christ
of Latter Day Saints

Herald Publishing House

COPYRIGHT © 1987
Herald Publishing House
Independence, Missouri
Printed in the United States of America

Library of Congress Cataloging-in-Publication Data

Troeh, M. Richard.
    The Conferring Church.

Bibliography: p.
Includes index.
    1. Church meetings.   2. Parliamentary practice.
I. Troeh, Marjorie.   II. Title.
BV652.15.T76   1987   262'.09333   86-18459
ISBN 0-8309-0465-4

94 93 92 91 90 89 88 87   1 2 3 4 5 6 7 8

TABLE OF CONTENTS

INTRODUCTION

This book has evolved slowly over a period of several years. We owe many people—more than we can name—for assistance in developing the concepts in the book, and for their encouragement when it seemed we would never get finished writing it.

Our concepts began when both of us heard stories about General Conference from older family members and friends who were able to attend from time to time. Marge grew up in California and Dick in Idaho, so most of these stories were about awe-inspiring, once-in-a-lifetime experiences for the participants. We could tell they were monumental events in the life of the church.

We personally observed our first RLDS General Conference in 1954 when we were students at Graceland College. Dick was able to attend part of the 1956 Conference when he was a student at Kansas University. We both attended part of the 1962 Conference when he was in the Army at Fort Riley, Kansas. We will never forget the warm hospitality of the Herman Basler family who furnished us housing, and even baby-sat our infant daughter so we could attend the meetings.

Our sense of awe continued throughout all of these Conferences as we saw the business of the church being carried out. Particularly inspiring was the opportunity to see some of the persons "come to life" who had previously been only names for us. Observing their participation made us realize they were "just people" like everyone else. Some were unforgettable. A member pointed out in debate of an issue that F. Henry Edwards had made a statement that contradicted something he had written several years earlier. President Edwards didn't try to explain away the contradiction. His response was simply that it would be tragic if he hadn't learned something in the years since he had written the earlier statement. The combination of intelligence, devotion, and humility in leaders such as this has inspired us on many occasions as we have seen them in action in Conferences over the years.

We moved to Independence in 1966, and since then have participated in every World Conference in varying capacities—observer, elected delegate, and as *ex officii*. Marge was Commissioner of Women's Ministries from 1971 to 1982, which gave *ex officio* status and a very active involvement in World Conference preparations and associated activities, such as the International Women's Forums, which were held before several Conferences. She has also served for a number of years on the Conference Organization and Procedures Committee, and on the World Church Peace Committee. Dick is a physician and high priest who has been very active in congregational and stake activities, and in the Quorum of High Priests at World Conferences.

The idea for this book arose out of church school classes in which we participated, and which we taught on several occasions. We first attended the East 39th Street Congregation, where Wilbur Sartwell led a class discussing "Conference issues" prior to the 1968 Conference. The class discussed what a Conference is, how one could participate responsibly, and also considered reports and legislation which were coming up at the Conference. Afterward, the class continued and discussed the significance of what had happened at the Conference, and the particular implications for our stake and congregation. We were asked to lead a similar class before the next Conference, and it became a routine expectation for the spring semester of World Conference years.

We moved to the Pleasant Heights Congregation after we had moved to a home in that area, and for several years participated in similar classes there. We developed a general outline for the class which could be repeated from one time to another. Many of the members of the classes contributed to this book as they participated in the discussions and gave ideas for improvement in future presentations of the class.

The "Conference issues" class came to the attention of the World Church Christian Education Commission a few years ago, and we were asked to develop it as a study guide for an adult church school class. We promptly set to work developing a detailed outline, which went through an initial editorial review process, including the First Presidency. However, we had outlined a resource much more comprehensive than could be contained in such a limited form, and we had to either scale it down or present it in another format—a book. When the book format was selected, the time requirements and need for consultations were multiplied.

The many people with whom we have associated in Conferences over the years have all contributed to the writing of this book. This includes especially those with whom we have discussed the nature and meaning of Conferences, and also with whom we have worked in writing and presenting legislation in several Conferences. As we have participated in the conferring process, we have become interested in understanding the theory and practices of conferring as carried out in the church, and often have reflected upon the opportunities within Conferences for expressing the values affirmed by the church.

These interests led Dick to present a paper to the Mormon History Association in 1985 about the legislative processes of the RLDS Church. An expanded version of the paper was published in the Fall 1986 issue of *Dialogue*, under the title "Divisions of the House: Legislative Processes of the RLDS Church, 1964-84." This paper specifically analyzed the types of legislation presented, the sources of the legislation and the methods by which it was introduced and handled, and described many of the happenings in World Conferences of those twenty years.

We have tried to carefully document in our references the writings of other persons who have informed us on the subjects we have covered. Undoubtedly, though, some of our ideas have come from materials we have read, or speakers we have heard, but can no longer remember or identify the source. We give thanks, therefore, to the many individual writers, speakers, and teachers who have influenced our understandings over the years. We owe particular recognition to a few individuals who have given us extra encouragement, discussed specific concepts with us, furnished us materials, or reviewed portions of the manuscript. These persons include Henry Livingston (with whom Dick held many rewarding discussions), Elbert Dempsey, Sharon Knapp, Richard Howard, Frederick Troeh (Dick's brother), Ruth Bradley (Marge's mother), Madelon Brunson, Lavina Fielding Anderson (who edited the *Dialogue* manuscript), W. B. (Pat) Spillman, and all of the members of the First Presidency. All have improved this work through their contributions, though they bear no responsibility for any remaining errors in fact or concept, which must be ours alone.

We hope that this book will be a useful resource for members who would understand the place of World Conferences—and also of other meetings for doing business—in the life of the church, and how they can share in the church's processes of doing business. We have attempted to make it useful for the preparation of individual delegates and delegations to participate responsibly in Conferences. We have tried to make it a handy reference, locating in one readable source information on the selection of delegates, preparation of legislation, parliamentary procedures utilized in the church, and the roles and responsibilities of presiding officers, delegates, and others. We envision it as useful either for individual or class study. To be used best, it requires access to some other materials as well:

The Holy Scriptures, Book of Mormon, and Doctrine and Covenants
Rules and Resolutions
Robert's Rules of Order
World Conference Bulletins—preferably for the last several Conferences
The History of the Church
Saints Herald

We hope that Conferences will be studied, not as ends in themselves, but for what they show about a church that is involved in doing God's business. As such, we hope the book helps to develop the understanding that Conferences are a form which needs to continually evolve to serve a necessary function—the process of decision-making in the church—and that how decisions are made is important as well as what decisions are made. If it helps some members to understand how to confer together responsibly as brothers and sisters in Christ, our purpose in writing the book will have been accomplished.

M. Richard and Marjorie Troeh

CHAPTER 1
Overview

KEY CONCEPT: As the body of Christ, the church is engaged in mission in the world; this mission requires organized effort to be accomplished; this in turn requires established decision-making procedures by the body.

The major reason for having a Conference is to conduct the business of the World Church. In the same sense that the world situation is a paradox of unparalleled opportunity and profoundly disturbing problems, the Conference must inevitably respond to the calling of a prophetic church and at the same time concern itself with the internal problems of growth. In both aspects of the task there is need to understand the significance of conferring together in a responsible manner.[1]

With these words in 1970 the First Presidency called the church "to change the format [of Conferences] in ways which more fully conform to expressed desires of the members,"[2] and accommodate to the needs of the church to accomplish its mission in the contemporary world. The changes in format which have followed, as well as the traditional patterns which have been retained, have had practical significance in the decision-making procedures throughout the church—at every level and in every jurisdiction. A basic understanding which has developed throughout this process is that formats and procedures must be *continually* reevaluated and adapted if the church is to express faithfully the timeless truths of the gospel within a rapidly changing world.

The church has been called the body of Christ (I Cor. 12:27, Eph. 1:22-23, Col. 1:18). This body is an association of individuals who have entered into a covenant relationship with God, becoming "no more strangers and foreigners, but fellow citizens with the saints, and of the household of God" (Eph. 2:19). The members are to be so close and loving of one another that they can be seen as *one* body (I Cor. 10:17), but this in no way means that all members should *be* the same (I Corinthians, chapter 12). In fact, Paul in the Corinthian letters indicates that "a more excellent way" is that the body has many members with "diversities of operations" (I Cor. 12:6).

The very diversity of its members helps the body to effectively carry out its many functions. It is essential to its mission that the church be a collection of committed individuals with diverse backgrounds, talents, and functions—but also that the same Spirit makes them care sufficiently for one another that when one member suffers all suffer, or when one is honored all rejoice (I Cor. 12:26). Thereby they are recognizable as one body.

To work together as one body, the various members act cooperatively toward a common purpose which is well enough understood by all that they may coordinate their efforts in one overall mission. The right hand must know what the left hand is doing, and by coordinating their movements the two hands may accomplish much more than either one alone. And if both coordinate with the feet, the entire body can have a balanced movement in the direction it should go.

The necessary type of coordination can occur in the body only with a functioning system of communication to and from the various members. Conferences are not the only way this communication occurs, but are an essential means by which the body determines its purposes and sets its directions for coordinated action.

The members of the church, if they are to be the body of Christ, will come together in particular ways and with particular attitudes in doing their conferring. They will come together prayerfully in the name of Christ, so that their actions may be appropriately consecrated (II Nephi 14:11-12). They will look to Christ "to be the head over all things to the church, which is his body" (Eph. 1:22-23). While Christ is the head, this does not mean that the members wait for his specific direction in all that they do. They are to be prayerfully and "anxiously engaged in a good cause, and do many things of their own free will, and bring to pass much righteousness; for the power is in them, wherein they are agents unto themselves" (Doctrine and Covenants 58:6d).

Those persons who exercise their agency *responsibly* choose God, and choose to love one another (Doctrine and Covenants 36:7b). In so doing, they take upon themselves Christ's nature and make his purpose their purpose. Christ's purpose is stated "to bring to pass the immortality, and eternal life of man" (Doctrine and Covenants 22:23b). This also becomes the overall guiding purpose of those who would come together corporately to be the body of Christ. The degree to which the church can accurately be known as Christ's body is determined by the degree to which this purpose is shown in Conference actions and elsewhere.

While an overall understanding of purpose is necessary for the church to act as one body, its mission can be couched only in terms of specific actions and programs if it is to be meaningful. As Christ made the word flesh, the church must continue to make the word flesh in every generation. Part of Christ's program for accomplishing his purpose was stated,

The Spirit of the Lord is upon me, because he hath anointed me to preach the gospel to the poor, he hath sent me to heal the brokenhearted, to preach deliverance to the captives, and the recovering of sight to the blind; to set at liberty them that are bruised; to preach the acceptable year of the Lord.—Luke 4:18-19

For the church to make the word flesh in the manner of Christ involves recognizing God's grace in each person, and

that there is a divine purpose implanted in every human life. The church must find itself binding up the wounds, feeding the hungry, and comforting the despairing wherever it goes, because this is the ministry of Jesus Christ.[3]

The needs of people provide the agenda for church programs. . . . Transformation of persons according to God's purpose for them is the goal.[4]

Being the body of Christ does not occur in isolation, but in community. The church must understand its need to recognize those forces in the community which are destructive, and those which are in accord with Christ's purpose. It must "come to grips with the appropriate role of the institutional church in influencing and directing the course of events in community, nation, and world scenes."[5]

We have been instructed to be involved with God in the educational, economic, political, and social life of our communities. We have always believed that he is at work in the world and will bring about through the instrumentality of his people and his church the kingdom of God on earth.[6]

As Arthur Oakman once stated,

We cannot shirk the task of influencing society....The church (supposedly) has special light and insight which we are called to bring to bear on the whole range of human relationships. If we fail to do this, and civilization founders, we shall have failed our Lord in the task assigned us.[7]

The magnitude of the task of being the body of Christ is tremendous. In spite of the immense task before the church, its resources are limited at this time for accomplishing that task. The church cannot be and do all things (even things that are good and desirable) in all places and times for all people. Exercising a responsible corporate stewardship requires that the church develop programs and activities which will expend its energies and resources as prudently as it can to best fulfill its mission in an ongoing fashion.

Prudence involves giving proper attention to the inner needs of the body, so that it will maintain a healthy life.

As a church we must maintain, at all costs, our own spiritual life. Although involvement in social work is important, we must not abandon the sanctuary entirely when we go out into the world. The spiritual life which the church generates nourishes the fellowship, which in turn gives power to the proclamation of the gospel in all its fullness.[8]

On the other hand, "a church without a policy for social action and ministry can hardly be called relevant."[9] If the church ignores the problems of violence, drugs, difficulties of family life, misuse of political and economic power, the injustices based on race, religion, age, or sex, and other social problems, it is not being responsive to the needs of people today. Conferences provide a forum in which the members of the body of Christ can confer and reach common understandings in setting directions and goals, and in allocating resources and energies, both to maintain the strength of the body and to move out in accomplishing Christ's mission in the world.

In a body of any substantial size, some system of formalized decision-making processes is necessary. The church follows democratic processes within God-given limits, and is therefore called a "theocratic democracy."[10] The Rules of Order describe this as being

not of human invention, but of divine appointment and origin. It was brought into being by command of God, is guided and administered by divine authority, is sustained by the light of the Holy Spirit, and exists for divine purposes; but notwithstanding the primary rights of Divinity in the church, God has committed to the Saints an important share in the responsibility of governing the church. "Neither shall anything be appointed unto any of this church contrary to the church covenants, for all things must be done in order and by common consent in the church, by the prayer of faith."[11]

The "theocratic" portion of the theocratic democracy is described as being expressed *through* priesthood, not *by* priesthood,[12] an important distinction. Also in regard to this concept, it might be noted that theocratic is an adjective while democracy is a noun;

thus the democratic aspects are modified by the theocratic modification of the definition. This is good, inasmuch as the explanation follows that probably if the church were strictly theocratic it would be ruled by priests and modified by democratic action. On the other hand, its democratic action must always be subject to tempering by its recognition of the priestly action which is of divine origin. This provides the basis for procedures to be initiated by priestly orders, but their final implementation is to be authorized by the people. In other words, the priestly initiation of policies and programs is subject to examination by the people under the principles of pervasive inspiration or what is legally known as common consent.[13]

The authority of priesthood members is meaningful insofar as they are first of all disciples and as they learn the will of God and make God's will their own. Only in this way can they properly interpret for their jurisdictions their perceptions of the mind and will of God, and identify the mission of the church in terms of human endeavor. This, too, involves the principle of common consent. All members have the responsibility to attempt to discern God's will for them in their life situations, and as their lives relate to the whole. God does not coerce in this process, but invites persons to use their agency responsibly as they confer to develop a collective understanding of God's mission for the church.

Arising out of the principle that "all things must be done in order and by common consent in the church" (Doctrine and Covenants 27:4c), the World Conference is recognized as the highest legislative body in the church. Provision is made for other conferences having to do with the common interests of groupings of members within specified areas.[14] At each jurisdictional level, from the World Church to the congregational unit, those who preside have the responsibility to give prophetic leadership in their appropriate areas. When the process of common consent has been followed (as in a conference) they are responsible for administering the work in such a way that the decisions of the body are implemented and its interests protected.[15] When so led, the body owes its responsible leaders its support, and should allow properly selected administrative officers to do their work without undue interference.[16] Only in this way can both elements of a theocratic democracy combine so that the unified body may accomplish the work entrusted to all.

Summary

The church, as the body of Christ, has many members with diverse functions, who should work together in a coordinated fashion as one united body. This requires formalized methods of decision making and communciating within the church. Balance is needed between expenditure of limited resources and time on inward-nurturing and outward-directed ministries. Creative responsiveness is needed, both to the leadings of God in scripture and current prophetic guidance through devoted and competent leaders, and in understandings developed among persons who have taken God's purposes as their own.

REFERENCES

1. The First Presidency, *Saints' Herald* (November 1969), 3.
2. Ibid.
3. Duane Couey, *Saints' Herald* (January 1969), 18.
4. Joe Serig, *Saints Herald* (May 1977), 21.
5. Clifford Cole, 1972 World Conference Address, *Saints Herald* (June 1972), 11.
6. Ibid.
7. Arthur Oakman, *Saints' Herald* (February 1971), 10.
8. Ibid.
9. Larry Pool, *Saints' Herald* (September 1969), 12.
10. Rules of Order II:6.
11. Ibid.
12. Rules of Order II:7.
13. W. Wallace Smith, 1972 World Conference Sermon, *Saints' Herald* (May 1972), 14.
14. Rules of Order III:15-21.
15. Clifford Cole, *Saints Herald* (November 1972), 11.
16. Rules of Order II:11.

CHAPTER 2
Conferences over the Years

KEY CONCEPT: Throughout the years of its existence, the church's conferences have adapted to the varying needs and developing understandings of the church in relation to its mission.

Regular conferences have been a central part of the life of the church at all levels since its organization. However, the nature of those conferences has changed dramatically in the more than 150 years since the first one was held in the Whitmer home in Fayette, New York. Changes have been evident in many ways—in location, frequency, and size, in the definitions of who may participate, the subject matters considered, the methods of conferring and making decisions, and the associated activities which occur with the conferences. Because of such variations, and the difficulty in defining just what a conference was in the early days of the church, it is impossible to state with certainty how many conferences the church has held.

The church was organized at Fayette, Seneca County, New York, on Tuesday, April 6, 1830.[1] The initial organization was simple, primarily limited to the ordination of Joseph Smith and Oliver Cowdery as elders. More complete organization was to be developed over the years as required by the addition of members and the receipt of further instruction.

Even early in its existence, the church had significant "light" on how to do business. The Book of Mormon had already been published, including the insight in Mosiah that

Now it is not common that the voice of the people desires anything contrary to that which is right; but it is common for the lesser part of the people to desire that which is not right; therefore this shall you observe and make it your law to do your business by the voice of the people.—Mosiah 13:35

At the organizational meeting, the people were asked to vote to accept their leaders and to approve the form of the organization. To the present day, the people of the church have continued to take this instruction to heart and to make their voices heard.

The first regular "General Conference" of the church was held on June 1, 1830, with a membership of about thirty.[2] There were several confirmations and ordinations, and a number of manifestations of the Spirit were described.[3]

The first few Conferences of the church centered around defining a system of beliefs and developing an organization, as well as most of the details of its functioning. Many baptisms, confirmations, and ordinations were performed at Conferences and the entire body defined the missions to be carried out by the church's ministers.

The church's second official Conference was held in September 1830, starting the practice over the next several years of holding them at intervals of about every three months. In the interval between the church's first and second Conferences, further instruction had been given through Joseph Smith that "all things shall be done by common consent in the church, by much prayer and faith; for all things you shall receive by faith" (Doctrine and Covenants 25:1b).

A similarly worded revelation went on to say, "neither shall anything be appointed unto any of this church contrary to the church covenants" (Doctrine and Covenants 27:4c). This instruction had become necessary due to a crisis in leadership, Hiram Page having claimed to receive for the church a number of revelations concerning church organization and the building of Zion. The Conference accepted the principle that the church has one prophet at a time who is authorized to receive revelations for the entire church. This point required reemphasis, however, in 1831, when it was reaffirmed through the church's leader "that there is none other appointed unto you to receive commandments and revelations..." and "that none else shall be appointed unto this gift except it be through him..." (Doctrine and Covenants 43:1b, 2a).

The church's third Conference was held on January 2, 1831, in Fayette, New York, at which time instruction was accepted (Doctrine and Covenants 38) concerning the work of the priesthood, the principle of stewardship, and the care of the poor, and also that the people should gather to Ohio. A gathering of twelve elders occurred the next month at Kirtland (not defined as a conference), in which a great deal of further instruction was given about the church's organization, several responsibilities of the priesthood, a number of aspects of financial stewardship, and how to handle judicial matters (Doctrine and Covenants 42).

At the church's fourth Conference, held in Kirtland, Ohio, in June, 1831, the first ordinations to the office of high priest were performed,[4] and instructions were given that the next Conference would be in Missouri (Doctrine and Covenants 52). The church was "moving" rapidly—organizationally, theologically, and geographically.

A Conference was held in Missouri on August 4, 1831, at the home of Joshua Lewis, a member of a branch which had been established in Kaw Township west of Independence. The day before, the place for a temple had been designated. The nature of other business at that time is not recorded, but during the month following that Conference, Joseph Smith presented a number of revelations, including what became Sections 59 through 63 of the Doctrine and Covenants.[5]

During the next few years, a number of regular and special Conferences were held at various intervals and in various locations in Ohio, New York, and Missouri. Some of these might not be considered "general" conferences, as they handled primarily local business and, except for a few top leaders who were able to travel to them, were attended only by people in a given locale. However, at a number of these Conferences, actions were taken on behalf of the entire church. They were usually regarded as "general" conferences if General Church leaders were present.

At a special Conference in November 1831, probably at Hiram, Ohio, Joseph Smith presented the preface for a "Book of Commandments." The Conference authorized him to gather together the revelation received thus far and arrange them so Oliver Cowdery could take them to Independence for printing by W. W. Phelps.[6] The selection was made, but the printing was never completed, due to the destruction of the church's printing press on July 20, 1833.

In a special Conference at Amherst, Ohio, on January 25, 1932, Joseph Smith was first ordained as president of the high priesthood.[7] This action was later ratified at a Conference in Missouri on April 26, 1832.[8] In February 1834, the Standing High Council was first organized at Kirtland "for the purpose of settling important difficulties, which might arise in the church." On July 3, 1834, a "High Council of Zion" was organized to perform similar functions in Missouri.[9]

A simultaneous General Conference and a meeting of the High Council of Kirtland was held in September 1834. A committee was appointed (consisting of Joseph Smith, Jr., Oliver Cowdery, Sidney Rigdon, and F. G. Williams) "to arrange the items of the doctrine of Jesus Christ," for the government of the church with the provision that, "These items are to be taken from the Bible, Book of Mormon, and the revelations which have been given unto the church, up to this date...."[10] On August 17, 1835, a "general assembly" of the church at Kirtland approved the work of this committee.[11] The vote was taken, "first by the quorums separately, and then by the assembly as a whole, and that in every instance by unanimous vote."[12] This was the first occasion on which an assembly of priesthood quorums of the church officially voted to accept the revelations of the prophet as scripture. This was done by affirming that the book (Doctrine and Covenants) was true, not by specifically reviewing the individual revelations. No further votes were taken to approve revelations during the life of the church's first prophet.

The first Quorum of Twelve in the Restoration was selected at Kirtland in early 1835. President Joseph Smith, Jr., indicated that the commandment was, "for the three witnesses of the Book of Mormon, to pray, each one, and then proceed to choose twelve men from the church, as apostles, to go to all nations, kindreds, tongues, and people."[13] After uniting in prayer, the three witnesses (Oliver Cowdery, David Whitmer, and Martin Harris) accordingly presented twelve names and the first apostles were promptly ordained. Soon thereafter, forty-five men were also chosen to serve in the church's first Quorum of Seventy, "to go into all the earth, whithersoever the Twelve Apostles should call them."[14] The organization of the church was becoming more complete.

The earliest Conferences of the church acted almost as "committees of the whole," under the strong leadership of Joseph Smith, Jr. They handled matters which have come subsequently to be regarded as "administrative" and "judicial." Conferences at that time voted on all types of business decisions, priesthood calls, sustaining of officers, missions for priesthood members, admonitions to members for their actions, and even on expulsions from the church. It is interesting that Conferences did not, however, vote on the revelations given by the prophet except for the one occasion on which they were approved for inclusion in the Doctrine and Covenants in 1835. As the quorums came into existence, they assumed many of the details of administering the affairs of the church which had been handled in the General Conferences. However, understandings of the proper roles and relationships of the various quorums and of the Conferences of the church had to slowly evolve over the years. (In fact, these understandings are still evolving.)

In March 1836, before approval by the entire body, resolutions were seen as requiring serial approval by the several quorums in the following order: deacons, teachers, priests, bishop of Kirtland, bishop of Zion, elders, high priests, seventy, High Council of Zion, High Council of Kirtland, the Twelve, and lastly, the Presidency of the church.[15] On this occasion, it was also noted that the records of previous Conferences were "imperfectly kept," and that there was need for improvement in record keeping. Actually, it is quite remarkable that Conferences were held so regularly, and records kept as well as they were, while the church was undergoing the severe difficulties with persecution and internal turmoil that occurred in Missouri, and later in Illinois.

The inner turmoil was significant, as shown by a Conference at Kirtland in September 1837, which refused to sustain F. G. Williams in the First Presidency, and also temporarily refused to sustain three members of the Quorum of Twelve. The three leaders publicly expressed repentance for the sins for which the Conference had rejected them, and they were then reinstated as apostles.[16] At a "general assembly" of the church at Far West, Missouri, in November, Williams was again rejected as a counselor in the First Presidency, after which the prophet presented four others to serve instead as "assistant counselors."[17] The voice of the people was indeed being expressed and heard.

As late as 1839, excommunications were voted in the General Conferences of the church. However, in April 1840, at a Conference in Nauvoo, it was determined that no further cases involving charges against individuals should be brought before Conferences, but should be handled by the proper administrative officers and quorums.[18] This decision was not always followed, though, for some time after it was made, at least with regard to perceived transgressions of some prominent leaders.[19]

General Conferences of the 1840s were all held in Nauvoo, except for an 1842 Conference in Kirtland later declared to be invalid.[20] The question of sustaining the prophet and the top quorums was regularly put before the Conferences. A number of stakes were formed with conference approvals, financial matters were decided, personnel in the various quorums were approved, and assignments of ministers were sustained. By the time of the martyrdom of Joseph Smith, Jr., on June 27, 1844, the numerical strength of the church was approximately 40,000 with about 30,000 living in and around Nauvoo.[21] Obviously, the ways of doing business in Conferences for a church of this size had to become far different from the meeting of thirty members at the church's first conference. The largest part of the church's business was done by the top priesthood leaders and quorums, with decisions by Conferences limited to matters brought to them by those leaders.

Though it was not a common practice in the early Restoration to vote on accepting revelations, those given through the prophet were used for guiding decisions. Seventy-three revelations were presented by the prophet through 1831, twenty-six in the next two years, but only eight in the next ten years. A logical reason for the diminishing frequency is that much more frequent and detailed instruction was needed in the formative years of the church than after the organization was more complete and functioning effectively.

In addition to instruction for the church as a whole, about half of the church's earlier revelations gave detailed instructions primarily directed to individuals. This may have occurred partially because of the church's affirmation of the doctrine of present-day revelation which was new to many people, and they naturally had the desire to see this gift expressed. The prophet was often asked for revelatory expressions of the Lord's will; this was frequently provided. Wise counsel was given in this regard in Doctrine and Covenants 58:

Behold, it is not meet that I should command in all things, for he that is compelled in all things, the same is a slothful and not a wise servant . . . Men [all persons] should be anxiously engaged in a good cause, and do many things of their own free will, and bring to pass much righteousness; for the power is in them, wherein they are agents unto themselves.—Doctrine and Covenants 58:6c, d

This instruction affirming human agency makes legitimate the imprint of individuals' personalities and desires on the decisions they make about God's will in their lives. This is just as true for the church's prophet as for other members. The style of government of the church bore the imprint of the personality of Joseph Smith, Jr., and with leadership changes after his death, it would be expected that changes in style would occur. Changes did occur because of the situations which were faced, but also because of the personalities of those who assumed leadership.

The church was thrown into great confusion at the death of Joseph Smith. Without generally accepted revelatory instruction on the matter of succession in authority, the organization was without a clear understanding of how to proceed. Over the next few years, a number of different individuals used varying rationales to make claims to be the church's rightful leader, including Sidney Rigdon, James J. Strang, William Smith, Charles B. Thompson, James C. Brewster, William Bickerton, Alpheus Cutler, and others. They all drew limited numbers of members to "conferences" which they called to confirm their claims.

The strongest initial claim to leadership, in terms of the numbers who gave support in a Conference, was that of the Council of Twelve. An emergency special Conference was held at Nauvoo on August 8, 1844, which passed a resolution "supporting the Twelve in their calling."[22] This was interpreted by them as authorizing the Twelve to preside over the whole church, with Brigham Young presiding as the senior member of the Quorum of Twelve. At first it was declared that Joseph Smith's place would not be filled,[23] but subsequently Brigham Young claimed the title of president and exercised strong and effective leadership for the portion of the church which went west to the Great Basin.

Two men who had been ordained elders in the original church became instrumental in bringing about the Reorganization. Jason W. Briggs and Zenos H. Gurley had briefly affiliated with some of the factions, but left them when they decided that they did not represent the original church.[24] In November 1851, J. W. Briggs recorded a revelation that

in mine own due time will I call upon the seed of Joseph Smith, and will bring one forth, and he shall be mighty and strong, and he shall preside over the high priesthood of my church; and then shall the quorums assemble, and the pure in heart shall gather, and Zion shall be reinhabited . . .[25]

Briggs' revelation was shared with several who were currently following James J. Strang, and convinced them that a son of Joseph Smith, Jr., should become leader. A Conference was called at Beloit, Wisconsin, in June 1852, with J. W. Briggs presiding. Several resolutions were adopted, including statements rejecting all claimants to the church's presidency except for the seed of Joseph Smith, Jr., recognizing the validity of previous ordinations in the church, and "that the whole law of the Church of Jesus Christ is contained in the Bible, Book of Mormon, and Book of Doctrine and Covenants."[26] "There was no intention at this time of organizing a new church, but these men were acting as members and officers of the original church, regulating and setting in order the church, according to the law...."[27] They acknowledged no head for the church, but stated their expectation for a head to come.

Those forming the Reorganization had started their wait for a son of Joseph Smith to lead them. It was an *active* period of waiting. A Conference was convened at Yellowstone, Wisconsin, on October 6, 1852, authorizing distribution of two thousand copies of a pamphlet entitled, "A Word of Consolation."[28] Another Conference convened at Zarahemla, Wisconsin, on April 6, 1853. At this Conference a committee was chosen to select seven men for ordination to the office of apostle. The Zarahemla Stake was also established.[29]

The budding Reorganization continued to hold Conferences, essentially on a semiannual basis throughout the 1850s. Their experience paralleled that of the earlier days of the church in many ways. Their numbers were small, and many details of functioning were handled by Conferences. These included approving calls and performing ordinations, baptisms, and confirmations, sustaining officers, designating ministerial assignments, and making decisions on financial matters and even on judicial matters. Votes were taken to recognize the baptisms and priesthood of many who had been in the church while the original prophet was living.

At a Conference held in the grain barn of Israel Rogers at Kendall County, Illinois, in October 1859, a resolution authorized the publication of a monthly church paper for a trial period of six months.[30] Thus, publication of *The True Latter Day Saints' Herald* was launched in 1860. The name has been shortened, but the *Saints Herald* has been published ever since.

A historic Conference was convened on April 6, 1860, at Amboy, Illinois. Joseph Smith III was present, saying

I came not here of myself, but by the influence of the Spirit. For some time past I have received manifestations pointing to the position which I am about to assume. I wish to say that I have come here not to be dictated by any men or set of men. I have come in obedience to a power not my own, and shall be dictated by the power that sent me...if the same Spirit which prompts my coming, prompts also my reception, I am with you.[31]

Isaac Sheen made the motion by which it was "resolved, that Brother Joseph Smith be chosen Prophet, Seer, and Revelator of the Church of Jesus Christ, and the successor of his father."[32] Truly, as reported in the Amboy newspaper, "A new era in the history of Mormonism has dawned."[33]

Semiannual Conferences continued throughout the 1860s and 1870s, at several different places, most often alternating between Amboy or Plano, Illinois, and a location near Council Bluffs, Iowa. Conferences also were held, however, at Keokuk and other locations in Iowa, and in St. Louis, Missouri.

The church continued to adhere to the pre-Nauvoo organization and doctrines as revealed through

Joseph Smith, Jr., as they were understood. But changing times and social situations called for continuing decision-making, and at times for further revelatory instruction, to carry the church beyond the forms and procedures that were appropriate to an earlier time. The early Conferences of the Reorganization also began dealing with some questions which either should have had attention in the earlier church, or would have had to have been dealt with even if Joseph Smith, Jr., had lived to lead the church for many more years.

Many of the issues dealt with by Joseph Smith III and his successors can be categorized:

  Church organization and administration
  Representation
  Location and frequency of Conferences
  Clarifying the doctrine and practices of the church

Church Organization and Administration

"Young" Joseph's leadership style *had* to be different from his father's. Sixteen years after his father's death Joseph Smith III assumed leadership of a people which included many who understood the original church's organization and proper functioning. They had already become more dependent on their own collective wisdom, expressed democratically after waiting for understandings to become pervasive within the group. They had seen the effects of false claimants to leadership, and were going to closely peruse the new leader's statements and actions, even if he *was* the long-awaited son of the original prophet.

Joseph III accepted the General Conference as the final authority in administering the affairs of the church, including the selection of its general officers. He soon recognized, however, that he had to work out a balance between the church's pattern of functioning democratically and its need for strong leadership. In the Conference of October 1860, he wanted to see the Quorum of Twelve filled (there were eight members), but the Conference accepted a committee report that only three men were qualified.[34] In March 1863, having consulted with the Lord about the need for a counselor in the First Presidency, he presented a revelation to the church that "It is my will that you ordain and set apart my servant William Marks to be a counselor to my servant Joseph, even the president of my church, that the First Presidency of my church may be more perfectly filled."[35] During the next several years, the committee method was again tried and failed several times to make selections to fill the church's leading quorums which had been depleted by deaths, inactivity, and a resignation. The democratic process alone was not enough to meet the leadership needs of the church.

The Conference of April 1873 helped to define the practice of "common consent" within the church. President Smith presented a revelation (Doctrine and Covenants 117), which filled the First Presidency (for the first time in the Reorganization), called seven new apostles (making ten in the quorum), filled the Standing High Council, called several to serve as seventies, and authorized counselors in the Presiding Bishopric. The Conference exercised the right to evaluate and endorse the document, but the precedent was established which has since been followed—that general officers of the church have been designated through revelatory documents presented to Conferences for their approval.

Joseph Smith III respected and jealously safe-guarded the rights of the people in applying the principles of common consent. Administrative actions were subjected to close legislative review by Conferences, to the point of dealing with fine details of the operations of the church instead of simply establishing general principles and goals.[36] The expression of personal opinions and feelings in Con-ferences was often outspoken, sharp, and acri-monious.[37] Shouting matches and (on rare occasions) even fist fights occurred. Judicial matters were often considered at Conferences and members expelled from the church by conference vote.[38] Some members of the Quorum of Twelve were not sus-tained on repeated occasions,[39] and at other times were publicly censured and admonished.[40]

An expanding and maturing church had to develop more effective and reasonable approaches to doing business, including distinctions among matters which were properly legislative, and those which were administrative or judicial. The Reorganization has had to deal continuously with the question of the rights of individual members in relation to the needs and rights of the institutional church. Though this question was of particular concern in the first thirty years or so of the Reorganization, it has persisted to this day.

Representation

At the Conference in April 1865, President Smith referred to the "necessity of making our conferences representative bodies."[41] The spring Conference of 1867 requested him to appoint "a committee of three . . . to draft or adopt a set of forms applicable to representation and the general use of the church."[42] The committee did not succeed in finishing its job. The Conference of April 1868, however, adopted a resolution "that all private members, male and female, have a right to vote on all questions that the elders may deem of sufficient importance to bring before the church."[43] In 1873, a district attempted to have the voting rights of women rescinded, and the Conference instead adopted a resolution admonishing the district, stating its action was "disrespectful to the entire body, and that said [district] conference is hereby respectfully requested to reconsider and rescind said resolution at their next quarterly conference session."[44] President Joseph Smith III was enthusiastic about the presence of women as delegates, at least in 1891 when he observed:

Our sister delegates to Conference . . . were representatives of the work, alive in their hope in Christ, and were both intelligent and well informed in regard to the faith and needs of the work . . . the votes they cast were on the right side—beyond a question. It was pleasant to know that they were there, watchful as well as prayerful.[45]

The Conference of April 1880 appointed a committee of five to prepare a system of representation to be presented to the next Conference.[46] This committee reported back, and the April 1881 Conference amended the recommendations and adopted the first rules for representation in the church. Provision was made for one delegate to the General Conference for the first six members of a branch, and one delegate for each additional twenty members.[47] The general officers of the church and ministers "under missionary appointment" were given ex officio status.

At the September 1881 Conference all high priests

and elders were given ex officio status, "and entitled to voice and vote when present."[48] During the next twenty years, various requests were repeatedly made, and turned town by Conferences, for priests, teachers, and deacons to be ex officii at Conferences. In this regard, it was also found necessary to define in 1901 that "the word 'elders' used in the law signifies those holding the Melchisedec priesthood only; all classes and orders of this priesthood are characterized by the word 'elder.'"[49]

In April 1882, the ratio of representation was simplified by changing it to one delegate per six members of a branch.[50] The 1884 Conference, however, changed the ratio to one delegate per twenty-five members, and also provided that a part of a delegation could cast the entire vote to which a district might be entitled.[51] It was also provided that one delegate could represent up to twenty districts. (Prior to this, a delegate could represent only one district.)

Nearly thirty years later, a committee on representation recommended to the Conference of 1911 a resolution which stated,

Whereas, the increased membership of the church already makes the conference delegation very large and less adapted to the transaction of business than a smaller assembly; and Whereas the church membership in the various stakes and districts is rapidly increasing in numbers; therefore be it Resolved, that the Rules of Representation be so amended that the rule of representation be based upon the membership of one vote for every 50 members . . .[52]

This recommendation was rather hotly discussed on repeated occasions. Action was finally taken at the 1913 Conference to accept a minority report of some members of the committee, but amending the ratio to one delegate per 100 members of a jurisdiction.[53] This ratio remained until 1980.

The next major change to the rules of representation was in 1964 after more than two years of extensive discussion. At that Conference, after consideration of multiple amendments, the *ex officio* status of elders was discontinued.[54] President W. Wallace Smith stated that Doctrine and Covenants 17:13 (given in the earliest days of the church) was "superfluous" to the church's current situation and did not conflict with the freedom of the Conference to determine its own membership.[55] *Ex officio* status was given to all appointees, high priests, and branch and congregational presiding officers. At many of the Conferences during the next twenty years, many resolutions were presented that would have restored *ex officio* status to all elders, but none was adopted.

The World Conference of 1982 made the next major changes in representation. *Ex officio* status was discontinued except for thirty of the church's presiding officers (the First Presidency, the Council of Twelve, the Presiding Bishopric, the presiding evangelist, the presidents of Seventy, the Presidency of the High Priests Quorum, and the church's secretary), with the proviso also that no *ex officio* could serve as an elected delegate. The ratio of elected delegates from the jurisdictions of the church will vary to keep the overall size of the World Conference at about 2800 members.[56] In 1984, this ratio was about one delegate per 68.4 members in a jurisdiction.

Frequency and Location of Conferences

As previously mentioned, the church in its earliest days held Conferences about every three months. The Reorganization, during its first thirty years, held

Conferences semiannually in a number of different locations in Illinois and Iowa. In 1881 Lamoni became the headquarters of the church until the move to Independence, Missouri, about forty years later.[57]

At the Conference in April 1882, a resolution was presented which read,

Whereas, The holding of the two General Conferences each year is attended with great expense, and in our judgment is unnecessary; therefore, be it Resolved, That when this Conference adjourns, it does so to meet April 6, 1883.

The resolution which was adopted allowed for an additional Conference in 1882, but provided thereafter for "notice being given through the *Herald* in regard to the change of time from semiannual to annual conferences. . . ."[58] The September 1882 Conference voted to adjourn to April 6, 1883, "and annually thereafter."[59]

The Conference of April 1883, held at Kirtland Temple, authorized the holding of annual reunions in place of the fall General Conference. The first of the church's annual "reunions" was held at Leland's Grove near Council Bluffs, Iowa, in September 1883.[60] Reunions near this site were considered the church's "general reunions," but soon thereafter, began to be held in many districts of the church. Reunions have since easily become "the most significant single feature of the fellowship of the Saints beyond that enjoyed in their home branches."[61] The idea for the first reunions arose out of disappointment at the lessened frequency of Conferences for meeting together in a fellowship. Freedom from having to do the church's business has allowed reunions to focus more on fellowship and the spiritual development of the Saints and to minister to many more people than would be possible at General Conferences.

During the late 1890s, discussions were held frequently on the advisability of holding Conferences every two years. In 1888, the Conference voted, 100 to 92, to meet in 1900 instead of 1899.[62] Following this, however, Conferences were again held annually through 1919, in Lamoni, Iowa. At the 1919 Conference, President F. M. Smith indicated it was time to move the church's headquarters to Independence, where all "general" and "world" conferences have since been held.[63]

The Conference of 1920 again decided that future Conferences should be held biennially (every two years), and authorized the president of the church to set the specific time and place.[64] Because of the frequency of inclement weather in April, the Presidency decided that fall, e.g., October, was the best time for Conferences.[65] The October 1922 Conference voted to return to annual Conferences,[66] but in 1923 it was determined not to meet again until April 1925.[67] Annual Conferences continued through 1930, but since then General Conferences have been on a biennial basis. The Conference of 1958 was held in October, but the other Conferences of the last fifty years have been held in the spring near the date of the birthday of the church. In 1984, the First Presidency recommended that the interval between World Conferences be changed to four years,[68] but this was turned down by the delegates,[69] and the frequency of World Conferences continues to be every two years.

Clarifying the Doctrine and Practices of the Church

Clarifying the doctrine and practices of the church, including a clear designation of writings regarded as scriptural, was of concern in the early conferences of the Reorganization. The Conference in October 1863 authorized a publishing committee for the church "to publish the Book of Doctrine and Covenants, with such corrections in arrangement as may be necessary."[70] The first edition published in the Reorganization was in 1864, and the committee included the revelations in the 1844 edition (published three months after the death of Joseph Smith, Jr.), as well as Sections 22 and 36 which had not previously been in the Doctrine and Covenants.

Specific conference approval was not given to further revelations in the Doctrine and Covenants until the September Conference of 1878. The Conference then affirmed

That this body...recognize the Holy Scriptures, the Book of Mormon, the revelations of God contained in the Book of Doctrine and Covenants, and all other revelations which have been or shall be revealed through God's appointed prophet, which have been or may be hereafter accepted by the church as the standard of authority on all matters of church government and doctrine...[71]

This Conference then approved Joseph III's revelations of 1861, 1863, 1865, and 1873 for inclusion in the Doctrine and Covenants.[72] Following this, the practice finally became fairly well established by which revelations were presented first to the quorums and orders of the church, and finally to the Conference for acceptance for the government of the church and for inclusion in the Doctrine and Covenants. These two actions have not always been automatically combined, nor have revelations always been presented first to the quorums. In 1885, inspired instruction was given openly to the Conference without being presented first to the quorums.

It was accepted to govern the church, but not voted for inclusion in the Doctrine and Covenants (as Section 121) until 1894.[73] At the Conference of April 1894, Section 122 was accepted to govern the church, but not voted for inclusion in the Doctrine and Covenants until 1897.[74]

The Conference of September 1879 further defined the authority of the church's scriptures, declaring

it is not the intent and meaning...to make a belief in the revelations in the Book of Covenants, or the abstract doctrines possibly contained in it, a test of reception and fellowship in the church; but that the things therein contained relating to the doctrine, rules of procedure and practice in the church should govern the ministry and elders as representatives of the church.[75]

The same resolution speaks against "prescribing dogmas and tenets other than the plain provisions of the gospel," and states

The elders should confine their teaching to such doctrines and tenets, church articles and practices, a knowledge of which is necessary to obedience and salvation; and that in all questions upon which there is much controversy, and upon which the church has not clearly declared, and which are not unmistakably essential to salvation, the elders should refrain from teaching.

The General Conference of April 1897, at Lamoni, was also a very important one in the history of the church. Total membership was recorded as 38,370, and there were 432 delegates. Section 124 of the Doctrine and Covenants was accepted, with provision for the filling of the Quorum of Twelve for the first time since 1844, as well as the selection of a presiding evangelist. Guidance was also given for the functioning of the seventy.[76] The years that followed were to show the need for clarification regarding the functioning of all of the leading quorums.

At the Conference of 1902, President Smith presented a revelation in a somewhat different form from those previously given. He described it as a vision, in which he saw certain persons in the quorums of the Presidency, the Bishopric, and the Twelve, and also a number of evangelists. The Quorum of Twelve accepted it by a divided vote of nine to three, two of them indicating they had no light on their calls as patriarchs as implied in the vision.[77] The vision was accepted, though, by the Conference as Section 126 of the Doctrine and Covenants.[78]

Also included in the 1902 revelation was further instruction about the law of tithing and the responsibilities of the bishopric. For a number of years, much of the responsibility for the management of the church's financial affairs had been carried by the Quorum of Twelve, without a clear definition of the role of the bishopric. The bishopric's role in financial matters was clarified somewhat in 1932, when the Twelve presented a resolution

that the Presiding Bishopric shall assume and are hereby directed to assume full responsibility to see that the finances of the church are used strictly in accordance with the laws and enactments of the church, and for the faithful performance of such responsibility they shall be held answerable to the church in General Conference assembled.[79]

Through the years, the relationship of the bishopric to other administrative officers of the church has continued to require clarification, right up until recent times, as indicated by the counsel given in 1968 as Sections 149 and 149A of the Doctrine and Covenants.

President Joseph Smith III died in 1914 and was succeeded by his oldest living son, Frederick Madison Smith. The imprint of a powerful, new personality was brought to bear on the church's administrative affairs. Also, the internal needs of the church and the nature of the world in which it existed called for new approaches to leadership under the new prophet. Joseph III had assumed leadership of a small and struggling group of Saints in a largely agrarian society. Though he did not seek such a degree of centralized authority, many members bypassed established administrative procedures and went directly to the president of the church, the obvious center of authority, with their problems, advice, and requests. This informality was possible particularly while the church was small, but was still expected by many even as it grew.

F. M. Smith, on the other hand, assumed leadership of a church of about 71,000 members (66,000 in the United States and Canada), in a society which was becoming more industrialized and complicated. The leading quorums of the church were already filled and functioning.[80] Simply due to the size of the church, he (and his successors) could never enjoy the informality and closeness with such a large proportion of the membership as did Joseph III. Administrative responsibilities clearly had to be shared more broadly and various administrative roles clarified in an organization which was larger, more complex, and more formal.

Significant differences in understanding their roles, particularly between the quorums of the First Presidency and the Twelve, came to light in the Conference of 1919. An impasse was reached, leading President F. M. Smith to offer his resignation as president of the church.[81] It was not accepted by the Conference, which instead voted to "express our confidence in him as prophet, seer, and revelator to the church and as the President thereof."[82]

Church headquarters was moved to Independence in 1920, and President Smith recommended building a "General Conference Auditorium" there that "should be an auditorium the capacity of which is not one less than seven thousand,"[83] predicting that a smaller one would be inadequate. He had estimated the church's needs very well.

Greater harmony was expressed in the 1920 Conference, but in the 1922 Conference, held in a "canvas tabernacle" (a huge tent holding 3,000) on the current Auditorium site, difficulties between the quorums were again expressed. Section 134 was presented first to the Conference as a whole, then referred to the quorums. The Quorums of Twelve and of the Seventy declined to approve the document, but the Conference voted to approve it, 656 to 452. Significant and moving statements of reconciliation and acceptance of the will of the body were then made on behalf of both the Presidency and the Quorum of Twelve.[84]

Differences of opinion regarding the functioning of the leading quorums peaked at the Conference of 1925, one of the most important Conferences of the Reorganization. During 1924, a "Document on Church Government" had been prepared by the First Presidency and published in the *Herald*.[85] The document had had extensive discussion prior to the Conference, with firm positions taken without much willingness to work out differences. The greatest difficulty was with regard to the term, "supreme directional control," found in the following statement:

God directs the church through clearly indicated channels (Doctrine and Covenants 43:1, 2; 27:2); and his voice is the directing power of the church; but to this the assent of the people must be secured. In organic expression and functioning there must be recognized grades of official prerogative and responsibility (Doctrine and Covenants 104; 122:9), with supreme directional control resting in the Presidency as the chief and first quorum of the church...[86]

President Smith made it clear in his address to the Conference that he accepted the General Conference as the highest legislative body for the church, but that there needed to be a clear distinction between legislative and administrative functions in its government.[87] The original document defining mechanisms of church government was adopted by a vote of about two to one. Soon thereafter, the Conference also accepted as revelation Section 135 of the Doctrine and Covenants.

A number of persons withdrew from the church, and some others who remained carried great bitterness long after the "supreme directional control" controversy. F. Henry Edwards commented on the situation as follows:

Looking back from the vantage point of the years it is hard to understand why general officers and others felt so deeply about the phrasing of the document on church government. It seems to be beyond doubt that if it could have been considered less passionately it could have been restated so as to preserve what was essential but eliminate phrases which were obnoxious. If this had been done, there is little doubt that the revised document could have been adopted with a large measure of unanimity.[88]

A willingness to reason together and to work cooperatively for the best legislative statements for the church will always accomplish more than the argumentative rhetoric and political maneuvering that come as people support their rigidly polarized preconceived positions. While all decisions are important, it is at times less important *what* specific decisions are made than *how* the decisions are made—with acrimony and political maneuvering, or with respectful and loving conferring. In the past it has occurred both ways. Understanding their history should help church members choose the better ways to make decisions.

In spite of the tensions which occur, it has proven better to identify and face problems squarely rather than attempt to ignore or to avoid them. It is best, of course, to handle problems in the proper forums, not seeking public airings for matters which can and should be handled more privately when a limited number of people are involved. When problems are of church-wide concern, however, they are best considered forthrightly in an atmosphere of open sharing of viewpoints and of respectfully conferring. This is the most likely way to achieve the best solutions possible for the church. After the serious differences in 1925, the Conferences in the decade that followed were filled with evidences of unity and rich fellowship. The Conferences of the 1930s were quite sober due to the financial difficulties experienced in the Great Depression, but the unity was great as the members were kept well informed and participated in the decisions made to handle the serious problems associated with the church's debt. F. Henry Edwards records that, "By the time of the Conferences of 1940 victory was in sight, and there was a sense of triumphant comradeship."[89]

By 1926, the currently familiar patterns of Conferences were pretty well established.[90] Selection of the First Presidency to preside and to establish the agenda has been routine, as well as opening formalities including displaying the flags of the nations where the church is established. Acceptance of the credentials of delegates on the basis of the Rules of Representation is a first order of business. Reports are presented (usually having been printed in advance) by the leading quorums and departments of the church. These reports often contain recommendations for legislative actions by the Conference. Many "housekeeping" items of business are handled at every Conference (as described in Chapter 3), the most important being the church's budget and sustaining of general officers. Then comes the legislation recommended to the Conference from various sources—jurisdictions, quorums, etc.—which is always handled better when delegates have participated well in the various quorum and delegate sessions. The evening services of preaching by general officers are also an integral part of the Conference, usually dealing with church policy and doctrine. Participation in the various adjunctive services, programs, and meetings is also important to experience the full benefit of a World Conference.

The forms of World Conferences in today's world bear little resemblance to the Conferences of the early days of the church, either in 1830 or of the Reorganization in 1860. But a consistent spirit is evident throughout the years of the church's Conferences—the spirit of a body of people "on a journey" with God to express the divine will in what they say and do together—a body of people given light from God, but nevertheless with the ability and responsibility to "bring to pass much righteousness" themselves "of their own free will," by reasoning and working together to make the most of their varied talents and understandings.

As the church has grown over the years, as the world has changed around it, and as the problems and opportunities for ministry have changed, the forms and content of the church's Conferences have had to change and adapt. Each generation has had to struggle with how to best express God's eternal truths in the changing world. Some Conferences stand out as being particularly significant and precedent-setting in defining mission—1830, 1835, 1844, 1852, 1853, 1860, 1873, 1897, and 1925, for example. If the church is acting prophetically—interpreting corporately the mind and will of God for its day—*every* Conference should be precedent-setting. Every Conference should find the people of God seeking and finding, in decisions made lovingly and intelligently, new and better ways to more fully implement God's way in what they say and do. History shows this *has* been done in many Conferences of the past, and *can* be done even better in the future.

REFERENCES

1. Church History, Volume 1 (Herald House), 77.
2. Church History, Vol. 1, 87.
3. Ibid., 123.
4. *Journal of History*, Vol. 1 (Herald House), 115.
5. *Journal of History*, Vol. 1, 116, 117.
6. Church History, Vol. 1, 221-225.
7. Ibid., 245.
8. Ibid., 247.
9. Ibid., 429, 503.
10. Ibid., 523.
11. F. Henry Edwards' *New Commentary on the Doctrine and Covenants* (Herald House, 1977), 33.
12. Church History, Vol. 1, 578.
13. Ibid., 541.
14. Ibid., 549.
15. Church History, Vol. 2, 28, 29.
16. Ibid., 107, 109.
17. Ibid., 117.
18. Ibid., 448.

19. Ibid., 572, 650.
20. Ibid., 551.
21. Church History, Vol. 3, pp. 1, 2.
   (Some estimates of the numerical strength of the church in 1844 were as high as 150,000 to 200,000, but these appear to be greatly inflated.)
22. Church History, Vol. 3, pp. 4, 5.
23. Ibid., 13.
24. Ibid., 196, 197.
25. Ibid., 201.
26. Ibid., 210.
27. Ibid., 211.
28. Ibid., 213.
29. Ibid., 218.
30. Ibid., 238.
31. Ibid., 247-250.
32. Ibid., 250.
33. Ibid., 253.
34. *Restoration Studies II*, 105. (Ref. *True Latter Day Saints' Herald* 1:236; Oct. 1860.)
35. Church History, Vol. 3, 318; Doctrine and Covenants 115:1b.
36. Church History, Vol. 5, 55.
37. Ibid., 47.
38. Church History, Vol. 3, 492.
39. Church History, Vol. 4, 286, 522.
40. Ibid., 478.
41. Church History, Vol. 3, 409.
42. Ibid., 468.
43. Ibid., 493.
44. Church History, Vol. 4, p. 5.
45. Church History, Vol. 5, 108.
46. Church History, Vol. 4, 310.
47. Ibid., p. 353.
48. Ibid., p. 366.
49. Church History, Vol. 5, 536.
50. Church History, Vol. 4, 392.
51. Paper prepared by Leonard J. Lea on "Conference Organization and Procedures," 1960, 32, 33.
52. Ibid., 44.
53. Ibid., 50.
54. 1964 WCB, 296-298.

55. Ibid., 297.
56. 1982 WCB; Rules of Order, IV:24.
57. Church History, Vol. 4, 373.
58. Church History, Vol. 4, 392.
59. Ibid., 405.
60. *Saints' Herald* 30:40 (Oct. 6, 1883), 633.
61. Maurice Draper, "Reunions," *Restoration Studies II,* 146.
62. Church History, Vol. 5, 442.
63. Church History, Vol. 7, 384.
64. Ibid., 390, 463; WCR 808.
65. Ibid., 464.
66. Ibid., 508.
67. Ibid., 565.
68. 1984 WCB, 235.
69. Ibid., 311.
70. Church History, Vol. 3, 333.
71. GCR 215, and Church History, Vol. 4, 238.
72. GCR 216.
73. Church History, Vol. 5, 266.
74. Ibid., 263.
75. GCR 222.
76. Church History, Vol. 5, 391f.
77. Ibid., 569.
78. Church History, Vol. 5, 567, 573.
79. Church History, Vol. 8, 178.
80. Church History, Vol. 6, 595.
81. Church History, Vol. 7, 330, 333.
82. Ibid., 334.
83. Ibid., 386.
84. Ibid., 480-493.
85. Ibid., 593.
86. Ibid., 628.
87. Ibid., 634-639.
88. Ibid., 655.
89. Church History, Vol. 8, 50.
90. Ibid., 46.

CHAPTER 3
Functions of Conferences

KEY CONCEPT: Conferences are the means whereby the legal and practical requirements for legislative functions can be achieved as a worshipful expression of the church's response to its mission.

What is a Conference? The question will never be fully answered, for the organization and the procedures utilized by Conferences require continual updating to meet changing needs. And an answer for one person or group may not be the same for another, for a given Conference will be experienced differently by various people. A member coming from Germany, Africa, or India (or even from Canada or California), will experience it differently from one who lives in the "Center Place" and has not missed a Conference in years. And each Conference will be different to those who attend many Conferences.

While the World Conference is primarily a legislative body,[1] experience has shown that its legislative processes are best carried out in the midst of some other significant functions:

1. *Symbolic.*

As the church expands geographically and numerically, the function of the World Conference as a symbol of the gathered community becomes increasingly important. The symbol of the community which gathers together for enrichment, direction, and renewal is rich and meaningful. Added to this concept is the implicit recognition that the community which gathers does so in order to enable itself to scatter into the world to witness to the redeeming love of God.[2]

A great degree of regeneration and commitment can result in the lives of individuals who participate in a large gathering which is seriously and confidently doing God's work.

2. *Fellowship.* A close fellowship permeates the body which achieves significant unity in understanding its purpose. "Through the fellowship of sharing, whether it be through worship or informal association, a sense of oneness is achieved which serves to bind the conferees together."[3] A close and caring fellowship is the primary difference between individuals who come to confer instead of debate, to reach a consensus instead of winning a contest of wills. A nurturing fellowship enables persons to participate creatively together in productive activity within the mission of the church.

3. *Worship.* A rich worship life undergirds all the church does if it is truly about the work of its Lord. Worship directs attention to the presence of divinity in the human situation, and calls the church and its members to their tasks in relationship to God and the community. Worship helps members keep their purpose in clear focus as they organize, set priorities in legislative terms, and move out to do God's work.

4. *Conferring.* Conferring together informs members about issues confronting the church and about the concerns and ideas of its various members.

The conferring function does not demand a legislative enactment or consensus; rather there is recognition of the need for openness and deliberation. This function, indeed, suggests that there are areas of concern which should not be made subject to legislation, and that a diversity of viewpoints is healthy and desirable. Where legislation is proposed, the conferring function demands openness and tolerance to all points of view; it insures that those with minority views are given the opportunity for expression and that those with majority opinions take the time to share theirs.[4]

Legislative functions of the church's Conferences are best carried out with a good understanding of the other aspects of church government. The government of the church necessarily includes administrative, legislative, and judicial functions.[5] "No legislative body can rightfully take to itself administrative or judicial functions."[6] Each aspect must function with due regard for the responsibilities properly assumed by the other aspects if the work of the body is to be accomplished most effectively.

Legislative assemblies *cannot* properly act as judicial bodies. Most judicial matters are necessarily private for the protection of the members involved. It would be destructive to air most of them publicly. Also, large groups in conference are too unwieldly to hear and weigh evidence in a given case, or to research and apply church law in specific judicial situations. The rights of the body are protected by the appropriate administrative officers who must function judicially according to prescribed procedures under church law. The body in conference *can* legislate properly with regard to establishing judicial *procedures* to be followed by church administrators within the framework of what has already been accepted as church law.

Administrative functions are essential to the ongoing life of the church. In its administrative functioning, the analogy of the church to a human body is most appropriate (I Cor. 12:27, Eph. 1:22-23, Col. 1:18). The various aspects of administration are assigned to persons with specific callings and abilities under the overall direction of the First Presidency, "who administer the affairs of the entire church."[7] As stated in the Rules of Order, "properly selected administrative officers must be allowed to do their work without undue interference."[8] It is impossible for a legislative body to handle the details involved in program development and implementation, or to anticipate all of the adaptations required in response to changing times and situations. The body, therefore, expresses its will to the administrators in terms of stated policies and procedures and budgeted programs. All of these are then to be carried out in detail by the appropriate administrators "in such a way that the decisions of the body are implemented and its interests protected."[9] In church administration, the rights of the body are safeguarded by several mechanisms which are described in the Rules of Order,[10] and also by the submitting of reports to subsequent Conferences. In reports, administrative groups account for the ways they have implemented the will of the body as expessed in conference actions.

Legislative functions are carried out in World Conferences, and also in various subordinate jurisdictions of the church. These include mission, metropole, stake, and district conferences, and branch and congregational business meetings.

These conferences meet at the call of the responsible administrative officers, at times and places determined by the bodies concerned, or in emergencies at times and places set by the responsible administrative officers. Every such conference has authority to legislate for those it represents as long as it does not usurp rights lawfully centered elsewhere.[11]

Within the parameters described above, and ideally in a setting of prayerful worship and a rich conferring fellowship, legislative assemblies at Conferences serve the following functions:

1. *Sustaining of Officers* to preside over the church in its various judisdictions and to administer the programs of the church within the guidelines established by the body and by scripture.[12] In addition to the obvious need for the church to be organized, it must exist among the nations of the world and under their laws as a legal entity. Though the church is "an unincorporated association generally throughout the world,"[13] in accordance with the laws in various locales and with proper advantages to be obtained, the church has incorporated in several areas of the world. (See the Articles of Incorporation in Appendices A, B, C, and D of *Rules and Resolutions.*) A corporate structure requires the designation of responsible officers, so the sustaining of officers has specific legal as well as other practical and ceremonial significance.

2. *Approval of a Budget.* A system of budgeting must be followed for the most effective use of the church's resources. The budget gives legal sanction for funding programs and authorization for expending funds by the appropriate administrative officers. By choosing what will be funded, the Conference is a significant part of the process of assigning priorities to the various programs which are seen as a part of the church's mission. The World Church has established policies relating to budgeting for its programs, and has requested that all jurisdictions of the church

also "follow the policy of operating on an approved financial budget."[14]

3. *Receiving of Reports.* Reports inform the body of the interconference actions of the quorums and administrative staff. They thereby assist in fulfilling the accountability of these bodies to the church by describing their response to the decisions of previous Conferences. They also often contain statements of those quorums' understandings of the mission of the church, thereby serving as counsel for the membership.

4. *Adopting Legislation.* In addition to sustaining officers, establishing a budget, and receiving reports, Conferences may adopt legislation regarding programs to be implemented, and policies and procedures to be followed by those who administer the programs. Also, statements of positions may be taken through resolutions which address issues and concerns, when the body feels these may be useful in reaching out into the community.

5. *Accepting Statements of Revelatory Experiences* which are presented by the prophet as the mind and will of God. (This function is reserved to World Conferences.) The principle of common consent is followed in examining new expressions of revealed insights against the background of existing scriptures and individual understandings of the members. Revelations should, of course, be expected to say something new—otherwise they would be an empty form.

In understanding the role of Conferences in the life of the church, it would be wise to keep in mind the following statement of the Conference Organization and Procedures Committee prior to the 1974 World Conference:

The church is called to live in the world witnessing to the redeeming love of God and is called to perpetuate in its own life the ministries it discerns in the life of its Lord, Jesus Christ. Every structural form the church takes must facilitate this basic function. Thus, at root, the World Conference is to be understood as an instrument of the church's mission. Its primary role is to facilitate the achievement of that mission. Ultimately, the validity of what it does will be determined by the extent to which the mission of the church has been served.[15]

SUMMARY

The legislative activities of Conferences are best carried out in the midst of a worshiping, richly fellowshiping, well-informed group of members who come together to confer seriously about doing the Lord's work. Legislative processes are necessarily separate from judicial and administrative processes, each being essential for the success of the church's mission. Legislative functions include sustaining officers, approving budgets, receiving reports, accepting revelatory statements, and adopting legislation. Proper legislation includes establishing programs, policies and procedures, and making statements on positions.

REFERENCES

1. Rules of Order III:16.
2. Anita Butler, *Saints Herald* (January 1976), 29.
3. Ibid.
4. Ibid.
5. Rules of Order 9.
6. Ibid., II:12.

7. Rules of Order II:10, D. and C. 104:4, 107:39, 122:1, 2.
   For a detailed description of the various functions of administrative persons, refer to the Rules of Order, section II, and the references to the Doctrine and Covenants listed therein.
8. Rules of Order II:11.
9. Clifford Cole, *Saints Herald* (November 1972), 11.
10. Rules of Order II:11.
11. Ibid., II:12.
    Also see III:15-21.
12. D. and C. 120, and Rules of Order II:10.
13. WCR 866.
14. WCR 1008.
15. *Saints Herald* (March 1974), 7.

CHAPTER 4
The Conferring Function

KEY CONCEPT: Conferring, with open sharing of ideas and concerns, is essential to the development of common consent, which is a unified understanding of purposes and a willingness to act concertedly for their achievement.

The democratic processes called for in the body of Christ go far beyond those usually found in the "secular" legislative assemblies. For the church to be a living incarnation of the message it professes, its procedures and structures themselves must reveal its affirmation. For example, the church in affirming the worth of all persons[1] should develop its deliberative structures and procedures in ways to receive the contributions and hear the concerns of the largest number of persons possible. This must be done consistent with accomplishing the necessary work on behalf of the body.

Certain words used frequently with regard to the deliberative processes of the church are *confer, consensus,* and *common consent.* Dictionary definitions of these words do not express their total meaning in the life of the church, but do provide a starting point:

Confer is derived from the Latin word *conferre*, meaning to "consult together; compare opinions; carry on a discussion or deliberation,"[2] or "to have a conference or talk; meet for discussion; converse."[3]

Consensus means "general agreement or concord,"[4] or "an opinion held by all or most; general agreement, esp. in opinion."[5]

"Consent" means "agreement in sentiment, opinion, a course of action, etc.; by common consent...applying to somewhat important matters, conveys an active and positive idea: it implies making a definite decision to comply with someone's expressed wish."[6] It "implies compliance with something proposed or requested, stressing this as an act of the will."[7]

Common consent is the basic principle which should underlie all of the church's decision making (D. and C. 25:1b, and Phil. 1:27). It involves a willingness on the part of the whole body to be aware of and respect the opinions and sensitivities of each member. Common consent may not mean that total agreement or full understanding have been achieved by all persons on all issues. It does mean that all viewpoints have been sufficiently considered for the body to take action. If all members have participated in the decisions, they can in good conscience support the decisions of the body.

Those who represent a majority opinion have no right to expect a minority to support decisions of the body unless the minority's viewpoints have been taken into consideration before the decision is made. However, once decisions have been properly made by the body, with due regard to the rights of all, members would do well to follow an admonition given the church leadership that "Their right to free speech, their right to liberty of conscience, does not permit them as individuals to frustrate the commands of the body in conference assembly" (D. and

C. 125:16b). There are appropriate times and places to express varying viewpoints, and minorities should be heard and respected—but when the body has made a decision, minorities should respect the body in turn and join in the responsibility of accomplishing the stated will of the body.

Those who exercise common consent think and feel together about responsibilities which they share. It combines the unique gifts of each individual and makes possible an increased response by persons to each other and to the divine will through the rightful expression of agency. This magnifies the sum of the parts when united in the wholeness of the group. It is the process of achieving mutual understanding rather than merely getting a majority vote.[8]

"The basic question is not 'What can I do to persuade an assembly to vote for my proposition?' but 'What is the will of God for us together at this time and under these circumstances?' "[9]

Seeking the will of God means being receptive when God enlightens—not waiting for an expression labeled "Thus saith the Spirit." It also means prayerful involvement in the process of interpreting those truths already given (and even reinterpreting them from time to time) as life situations change. Common consent is to be achieved "by much prayer and faith" (Doctrine and Covenants 25:1b).

"Much prayer" as an element in common consent means worship, thoughtful study of the scriptures, awareness of our history, understanding of the present, and concern for the future. "Faith" as an element in common consent means trust in God, confidence in his purpose, and mutual respect for each other![10]

In certain respects, achieving a consensus could be regarded as the ultimate in common consent. Consensus essentially means full agreement by a body rather than a majority vote, and is desirable for a body that would act in a unified way toward a common goal. Consensus, however, is a more passive concept than "consent," being primarily a matter of a shared opinion. Consent is more active, more a matter of positive decisions resulting in action toward definite goals. The ideal might be stated as participating in the process of common consent to achieve consensus by the members of the group.

Common consent and consensus are impossible to achieve except in a setting of conferring. Conferring, at its best, involves a sharing of experiences, ideas, and concerns in an open and non-judgmental fashion among persons who trust one another's motives and goodwill. There is a world of difference between the situation in which brothers and sisters at conferences are seen as friends or as adversaries. Adversaries contend with one another to win support for their competing agendas. But friends can be assumed to share the same basic laudable goals and just need to work on achieving them together.

Common consent and consensus can be achieved only when sufficient conferring has occurred for the body to develop common understandings of goals and methods. Good conferring does not "just happen," however. It takes careful preparation, and an active commitment to the process by all who take part. Participants need to develop skills in presenting information and opinions logically, succinctly, and honestly, and to participate whenever they can add to the information to be considered before making a decision. They likewise need to develop their listening skills, which is often much more difficult. They need to listen *actively* while others are speaking, trying to understand and appreciate the viewpoints, concerns, and feelings which are expressed. Those who preside have the responsibility to serve as *facilitators* of the process of conferring, to assure that as many viewpoints as possible are allowed (and encouraged) to be expressed while attempting to achieve unity and common consent.

The result of open and effective conferring will usually be far better than the understanding or viewpoint held by any one part of the body prior to the process of conferring. By the process of conferring, unity can be enriched even *because* of diversity, when a variety of backgrounds and perspectives and insights expand the richness and depth of understandings of the entire body. These principles are evident in the prayer of Reed M. Holmes, then presiding evangelist, given at the close of the 1974 World Conference:

Our Father, We thank thee for this week of sharing, growth, and restraint—and for the swelling, heart-pounding sense of joy we have experienced.

Keep us reminded that the profusion of varied patterns and colors in thy garden exist side by side without clashing.

Indeed, the very diversity enhances the beauty and the rose does not look upon the cornflower with disdain, nor expect it to look more like a rose.

It is only among us, thy human creation, that beauty is shattered by diversity. Forgive us the foolish pride by which we justify ourselves while depreciating others.

Reconcile us to thee that being drawn to thee we shall find ourselves drawing toward each other and discovering the joy of singleness of heart.

Speak peace to our troubled souls. Beyond this, help us to speak peace to troubled souls and to refrain from words of accusation.

Quicken our sense of heritage—for it is there we come to some knowledge of who we are.

Stir up our motivations so that we shall sharpen our skills and make them available to thee.

Bend us gently but surely to thy will.

Renew our awareness that we are called and commissioned and need therefore to act and live as those who share labor and joy with thy Son.

Bless thy people, Lord, and through them, bless others. In Jesus' name. Amen.[11]

SUMMARY

"Conferring" involves open and nonjudgmental sharing of ideas and concerns. "Consensus" means that a general agreement has been reached. "Common consent" means an actively supportive participation by the membership in a course of action whether or not complete consensus has been achieved. It involves decision-making only after proper consideration has been given to the various viewpoints and concerns existing within the body. Support by minorities is properly expected only if they have first been heard, but their support should then be given. Diversity of backgrounds and viewpoints can enrich the depth and breadth of the understandings of the group and result in better decisions and courses of action *because* of the diversity.

REFERENCES

1. D. and C. 16:3.
2. *The American College Dictionary.*
3. *Webster's New World Dictionary of the American Language.*
4. *The American College Dictionary.*
5. *Webster's New World Dictionary of the American Language.*
6. *The American College Dictionary.*
7. *Webster's New World Dictionary of the American Language.*
8. Robert Bruch, "The Decision-Making Process," *Saints Herald* (February 1976), 35, 36.
9. The First Presidency, "Common Consent and Parliamentary Procedure," *Saints Herald* (March 1974), 3.
10. The First Presidency, *Saints Herald* (March 1974), 3.
11. Printed in the *Saints Herald* (May 1974), 16.

CHAPTER 5

Representation

KEY CONCEPT: In order to do business effectively, the size of a World Conference must be limited. A representative (delegate) system is therefore required; effectiveness depends on careful selection of delegates, and their responsible preparation and participation.

World Conference is the highest legislative body in the church and, as such, must be organized with reference to this function. The body should be small enough to function as a true deliberative assembly, yet large enough to allow for the expression of wide-ranging points of view. The Conference structure and how it relates to this function must be continuously examined in light of the concept of the church as a theocratic democracy and historic emphasis on the role of common consent in the decision-making process.[1]

The ideal is that the number of persons participating in a conference be large enough that all points of view are present, but small enough that all can be heard properly in the conferring process. The ideal, of course, is impossible to attain, but should always be a goal to be approximated as closely as possible. In relation to this goal, the church has adapted ways of coming together in conferences to perform the legislative functions involved in being the body of Christ.

Because of the number and dispersion of church members throughout the world, the World Conference is necessarily a delegate conference. The goal of the delegate system is, as previously stated, to limit the number of persons involved so that all may be able to engage in the conferring process and to allow business to be conducted in an orderly fashion. It is also an attempt to provide for proportionate representation for the various jurisdictions of the church regardless of their distance from the location of the Conference. It is hardly appropriate to term a conference a "World Conference" if large numbers of participants from the central areas numerically overwhelm the numbers coming from distant jurisdictions.

Basis of Representation

The "Rules of Representation"[2] of the church provide for two categories of membership in World Conferences—ex officio and elected delegates:

Ex Officio means "by virtue of office or official position."[3] The ex officio status of some persons, because of their resonsibilities within the church as administrators, is essential to the legislative functioning of the body. For example, the First Presidency (and in rare cases the Council of Twelve) must preside.[4] "The functioning of the quorums, councils, and orders is considered important to the World Conference; they shall have access to the Conference through their presiding officers."[5] The list of ex officii, therefore, includes "Members of the First Presidency, the Council of Twelve Apostles, the Presiding Patriarch, the Presiding Bishopric, the Church Secretary, the Presidency of the Quorum of High Priests, and the Presidents of Seventy."[6] There are thirty potential ex officii at each World Conference. They are not eligible to serve as elected delegates from any jurisdiction.

Elected Delegates are entitled to represent their jurisdictions with voice and vote in conference sessions.[7] They are elected[8] in appropriate jurisdictional conferences or business meetings (of stakes, metropoles, districts, national churches, tribal churches, and branches not included in these jurisdictions) prior to the World Conference.[9]

The number of delegates to the World Conference shall be apportioned to approximate a total of 2,800 persons. Each stake, metropole, district, national church, and tribal church shall be entitled to two delegates. Each branch not included above shall be entitled to one delegate. Additional delegates, in number adequate to bring the total to approximately 2,800, small be apportioned among the jurisdictions according to their membership enrollment.[10]

This procedure safeguards the right for every jurisdiction, however small, to have representation at the World Conference.

As a practical matter, many jurisdictions which are small or at a great distance from the location of the conference are unable to select delegates who live in their jurisdictions who can afford the time or the financial investment required to travel to the World Conference. It is, therefore, not required that all delegates live within the jurisdictions which elect them. In fairness, the delegations should, insofar as possible, represent the spectrum of interests and concerns within the jurisdiction from which they are elected. The individual delegates should become knowledgeable about the jurisdictions they represent. The extent to which the World Conference can make decisions with validity for the World Church is limited by the extent of its representation from throughout the entire World Church. If the Conference is to speak appropriately for the entire church, the decisions it makes must reflect the participation of all elements of the church in those decisions.

Alternate delegates may be elected to provide for the event that a properly elected delegate is unable to attend the conference.[11] The seating of an alternate within a delegation is for the entire duration of the conference, not on a session-by-session basis within a conference period.

Qualifications for Delegates

"The only qualification for eligibility as a delegate to the World Conference shall be membership in good standing in the church."[12] Any member of the church is understood to be "in good standing" whose membership status has not been modified by judicial action.

Proposals have been made from time to time to further define "good standing" to include such requirements as filing of tithing statements, paying tithing, abstaining from tobacco or alcohol, etc. While these are important and desirable personal standards for Saints, it would be impossible to enforce them throughout the church as standards for the selection of delegates. Also, since "all have sinned, and come short of the glory of God" (Romans 3:23), this should put the church in the position of listing which sins are disqualifying for a delegate and which are not. Certain aspects of falling short of perfect sainthood (if this term could be adequately defined) could be more serious than others, but also be less obvious and more difficult to measure. This would be unfair to members disqualified as delegates due to problems on the list, while others could become delegates who fall equally as short, but qualify because their "problems" are not on the list. Because *all* fall short of perfection, and conferences cannot adequately further define or measure "good standing," further legislation in this regard would seem to be futile. The First Presidency has uniformly ruled such attempts out of order on the World Conference floor, as being contradictory to the instruction given in Doctrine and Covenants 125:9. It would seem more fruitful to rely on the good judgment of the members of the various jurisdictional conferences to elect responsible delegates than to further define "good standing."

The foregoing discussion notwithstanding, the personal characteristics of candidates for delegate are a valid consideration to those who select them. Though the only legal requirement for participation in the business of the church is "membership in good standing,"

it is not reasonable that those who are not fully active in church affairs should be the legislative force of the group; therefore one's voice and vote should be backed with the support of regular saintly participation in the Zionic movement.[13]

It is therfore appropriate to consider the level of activity of candidates when selecting delegates. Other personal factors to consider are openmindedness, the ability to weigh issues, the willingness to prepare by study and prayer, and the willingness and ability to participate with others in conferring situations.

Delegations should include, insofar as possible, persons who are representative of all aspects of the jurisdiction. Proper considerations include age, sex, various viewpoints, various functional responsibilities, priesthood status, and others. Political maneuvering to select only one type of delegate in a delegation (e.g., representing only one philosophy) is incompatible with Christian behavior. It denies the equal worth of the other members of the jurisdiction. Members should rise above simply voting for their friends or for those of like viewpoint. "All are called according to the gifts of God unto them" (D. and C. 119:8), and the body is incomplete without the presence of *all* of its segments. Only when the body appreciates that all of its members are necessary, and provides for their presence, can it truly be called the body of Christ (I Corinthians, chapter 12).

Voting in Conferences

All delegates and *ex officii* are equally entitled to voice and vote in World Conference legislative sessions. Voting is usually by secret ballot for sustaining general officers and for elections to boards and committees. Most other votes are of a simple "Yea" ("Aye") or "Nay" nature indicated by a show of hands, a voice vote, or by standing. If the process of conferring has produced a consensus or near-consensus, this method is adequate.

If the result of a vote is not obvious to the presider or to a member of the conference, a "division of the house" may be requested. In this case, the negative and affirmative votes are counted. This method is usually sufficient to determine the majority will. It is time consuming, and should be called for only when the will of the body is in doubt so that the time can be used to the best advantage.

If these voting procedures are not decisive, yet another method exists by which a vote may be legally taken. This involves a complicated procedure by which delegations are polled individually. In this polling,

The delegates present at World Conference shall be entitled to cast the full vote of the areas which they represent. In case of divergence of views among the members of any delegation, the vote of the area shall be divided in the same proportion as the members of the delegation are divided.[14]

In the poll of the delegations, certain delegates could be entitled to cast up to twenty votes if they were to be elected as a delegate by twenty different jurisdictions, but "No delegate shall be entitled to cast more than twenty delegate votes in the same Conference."[15] The votes of *ex officio* members would be added to those polled in the delegations and a decision recorded. (There is no validity to the oft-repeated statement that the number of votes tallied from the polled delegations would be multiplied by 100 before adding the tally of the *ex officio* votes; except for proportionate weighting of votes within delegations, each vote of a delegate or an ex officio member of the Conference would count the same.)

This last voting procedure would be extremely cumbersome, time-consuming, and easily open to error in counting and calculation. Though such a vote might be *legal,* it is very doubtful if a close vote by this method could be said to truly represent the will of the body. It could not properly be described as having been arrived at by "common consent." Its use would indicate a serious lack of unity. It would probably be better to make no decision at all than to arrive at one by such a method. Whereas one side might "win" according to the outcome of such a weighted vote, *all* portions of the church would lose from the failure to achieve common consent. Remembering the instruction that "all things shall be done by common consent in the church" (D. and C. 25:1b), the body instead would best turn its attention to considering its need for unity by trying to achieve consensus or common consent through more conferring.

Though delegates are selected by jurisdictions and are seated at World Conference according to the jurisdictions which selected them, each delegate is to act for the benefit of the church as a whole. Delegates have a responsibility to be sure that the viewpoints and concerns of their jurisdictions are presented in the process of conferring. They should listen to the concerns of others, and then vote according to their own best judgment.

No jurisdiction may instruct its delegates how to vote on a given issue. Delegates should engage in the process of conferring and decide how to vote only after listening to and honestly considering as many viewpoints as possible on a given issue. If conferring did not take place before decisions, a "conference" would be unnecessary and futile—jurisdictions could simply be polled on lists of issues.

The actions leading to a successful World Conference for the church begin with the membership as a whole. If they are primarily concerned with fulfilling God's purposes in their daily living and church activities in their part of the world, they will select delegates who personally reflect this attitude. They will realize the worth of all persons and select those who are representative of the various characteristics, concerns, and viewpoints present. They will make these delegates aware of their own concerns and opinions, and then trust them to confer and legislate responsibly on their behalf. They realize that their jurisdiction is just one part of the church and that their delegates and their entire jurisdiction must act for the benefit of the church as a whole.

SUMMARY

The World Conference should have representation of all aspects of the church membership, but be small enough to do business effectively. Each jurisdiction has representation, with the total number of delegates about 2,800. In addition thirty World Church leaders are *ex officii*. The only required qualification is to be a "member in good standing," but delegates should have the personal characteristics needed to be responsible participants. While various methods of voting are possible, the simplest is adequate when consensus or common consent has been achieved. All delegates are to confer and vote not just for the interests of their own jurisdictions, but for the benefit of the entire church.

REFERENCES

1. Anita Butler, *Saints Herald* (January 1976), 30.
2. Rules of Order IV.
3. *American Collegiate Dictionary.*
4. Rules of Order III:18.
5. Ibid., IV:22.
6. Ibid.
7. Ibid., IV:23.
8. WCR 936.
9. WCR 1106.
10. Rules of Order IV:24.
11. Ibid., IV:23 and 26.
12. Ibid., IV:25; D. and C. 125:9.
13. *Church Members Manual* (Herald House), 87.
14. Rules of Order IV:27.
15. Ibid.

CHAPTER 6

Functions of Quorums and Orders

KEY CONCEPT: The quorums, orders, and councils of the church make valuable and distinctive contributions to the legislative process and the achievement of common consent.

While the primary responsibilities of the quorums, orders, and councils of the church involve the continuing administration of the church's affairs, they do have some important legislative functions as well. Some of these functions are obvious; others are more "behind the scenes," but still essential to the legislative processes. Some functions are shared by all of the quorums, but many are also specific to their respective quorums or individual leadership positions. These include essential leadership, support, educational, and advisory roles. Each of the presiding quorums, either directly or through their staffs, may serve as a resource to the Conference by furnishing needed information to the body before decisions are made. This information may be either simply factual, or counsel as to the anticipated effect of a given action on the church's programs. Each of the quorums, orders, or councils may also initiate legislation and present it to the World Conference. There are additional specific functions in the legislative processes including the following:

1. Members of *The First Presidency* have the most visible and active involvement in the legislative process: they preside,[1] establish and guide the agenda (with the assent of the body), and they may call special conferences if necessary.[2]

2. *The Council of Twelve* "is the second quorum in authority and importance in the general work of the church."[3] It presides in the absence or disqualification of the First Presidency.[4]

3. *The Presiding Bishopric* exerts a significant influence on the legislative process, primarily in advance of conferences, by its involvement in the development of the budget and financial reports which are presented to the body.

4. *The Joint Council* does not refer to any specific legal entity within the structure of the church. Any combination of councils within the church is termed a "joint council." The most frequently convened and referred-to joint council consists of the First Presidency, the Council of Twelve, and the Presiding Bishopric. Members of these quorums make a great deal of preparation for the World Conference. This includes preparing recommendations for programs requiring legislative enactment, administrative procedures requiring conference approval, seeking out qualified nominees for the boards and committees to be elected or approved by the Conference, and much work on the budget. Several of these quorum members are on the Board of Appropriations and expend a great deal of time and energy in preparing the World Church budget for presentation to the delegates.

5. *The* Quorums *of High Priests* and of *Seventies,* and the *Orders of Bishops* and of *Evangelists-Patriarchs* have no scripturally required legislative functions other than those already mentioned, but perform useful services by meeting and conferring before and during World Conferences. They often discern the concerns and desires of the various portions of the body and develop legislation to present to the Conference which brings together varying viewpoints.

6. *Mass meetings of the elders and of the Aaronic priesthood,* and *delegate caucuses* are formed at each World Conference.[5,6] They have no continuity from Conference to Conference, but while World Conferences are in session they function in much the same way as quorums—conferring about reports, proposed legislation, etc., and introducing legislation to the World Conference on the vote of the members of the mass meetings or caucuses who are delegates to the World Conference. Nondelegate elders and Aaronic priesthood may participate in the meetings, but only the delegates may vote.

By tradition, revelatory documents have been presented to the quorums, orders, and councils (and more recently to the mass meetings of elders and Aaronic priesthood) for their consideration prior to being brought to the Conference as a whole. By conveying the results of their deliberations to the larger body these groups have often been able to assist in careful consideration of the documents. In regard to initiating carefully thought-through legislation and considering revelatory documents, the quorums, orders, and councils have the advantage of being groups small enough in size to engage in the conferring process more effectively than the Conference as a whole.

In addition to the functions described above which typically occur in relation to every World Conference, there are some *potential* added functions of the quorums, orders, and councils. "In addition to the specific quorum functions indicated...the law provides for 'a convocation of the priesthood organized as quorums.'[7] This is known as a general assembly.[8] Membership in such an assembly would include the First Presidency, the Council of Twelve, the Quorums of Seventy, the Standing High Council, the Presiding Evangelist, the Presiding Bishopric and the Quorum of High Priests."[9]

The nature of the World Conference is related to that of the general quorums and the general assembly. In this connection it is important to note that the First Presidency, the Council of Twelve, and the Quorums of Seventy have responsibility in protecting the rights of the people (D. and C. 126:10d, e), and that they and other General Officers must act if the church or any portion of it shall fall into disorder (D. and C. 122:10a, c). The quorums of the church are authorized "to decide concerning the law in the church articles and covenants" (D. and C. 119:7a), and "the several quorums which constitute the spiritual authorities of the church" (D. and C. 104:11j) are to pass on the decisions of the Presidency, Twelve, and Seventy if it should be alleged that these decisions have been made in unrighteousness.[10] The church has been blessed inasmuch as these safeguards have never had to be invoked. While the organization and functioning of a general assembly would be cumbersome, and fortunately has been only a theoretical possibility in the history of the church, these provisions in the law safeguard the rights of the body if serious disorder were to develop.

All members of the general quorums, orders, and councils have an awesome responsibility to the church and to the people who look to them for leadership. Each is seen

as a part of a leadership team of the World Church and as a representative of the World Church...charged with the task of faithfully interpreting the objectives and programs of the World Church to members as well as to those beyond the household of faith [and to] represent the church as ministers and as administrators in organizing and empowering the church to move forward in its mission.[11]

SUMMARY

The quorums, orders, and councils are primarily responsible for the continuing administration of the affairs of the church, but they also have important legislative functions. These include presiding over, conferring with, informing, and recommending legislation for the World Conference. If necessary, they could meet in a general assembly to safeguard the church in the event of serious disorder. In addition to the standing quorums, orders, and councils, at each World Conference mass meetings of elders and Aaronic priesthood function in much the same manner as quorums.

REFERENCES

1. Rules of Order III:18; World Conference Resolutions 386, 849.
2. Rules of Order III:20.
3. WCR 386.
4. Rules of Order III:18.
5. WCR 1125.
6. WCR 1169.
7. Rules of Order III:17; D. and C. 85:19b, 36a; 92:1e, f; 108A.
8. Rules of Order III:16, 17.
9. D. and C. 104:11.
   "From the First Presidency," *Saints' Herald* (January 1970), 3.
10. "From the First Presidency," *Saints' Herald* (January 1970), 3.
11. Clifford Cole, "Prophetic Leadership—A Continuing Need," *Saints Herald* (November 1972), 10.

CHAPTER 7
Reports

KEY CONCEPT: Reports to Conferences are key sources of information regarding the progress and current status of the church in its mission, and represent an accounting of responsible administrative officers to the body they serve.

Reports by those with responsibilities on behalf of the church have always been a significant part of Conferences. When the church was small, legislative activities took only a small part of the time of Conferences.[1] Missionaries' reports were a source of inspiration and strength, giving the assurance that the church was advancing in its mission, as well as noting where it was struggling.

A number of the resolutions of the early Reorganization concerned the reporting responsibilities of leaders and jurisdictions. In 1857, GCR 25 stated, "That it shall be the duty of all who are connected with us, holding priesthood, to report themselves personally or by letter once in six months, showing their faith and labor in the work."[2] Reports were also called for from all of the church's districts and branches. Though most of the attention of the church as a whole (and in this book) relates to the reporting function at the World Church level, the same principles apply to reporting at every level.

In the early days of the Reorganization, many of the church's missionaries were working almost autonomously in many places, having gone "without purse or scrip," receiving their sustenance from the field, and having little contact with the main body of the church. The 1892 Conference addressed this problem again, noting that

a man may be well known as a minister, and may have been engaged in the mission field for years, yet in the absence of anything in the shape of a report or statement direct from him, as a matter of record, he may be left out, and undoubtedly will be. . . . Do not forget that next March, as early as the 25th, we will expect reports from all missionaries to those in charge.[3]

This same Conference, however, noted that the church's growth, and the number and length of reports had become too great for delegates to handle. They instructed that reports to General Conferences be made primarily by General Church officers, and that other reports be made to the appropriate administrative persons on behalf of the church.[4]

The Conference of 1914 further defined reporting methods within the church.[5] Some departmental heads had felt that they were responsible to the First Presidency in a secondary way only, and that they had the right both to report directly to the General Conference and to ask for conference approval of matters not approved by the Presidency. It was made clear, however, that the church's departments would report to the First Presidency, under whose direction they worked, and through the Presidency to General Conferences. It was also clarified that committees, quorums, etc., of local jurisdictions would make their reports to their local conferences and administrators.[6] These procedures are clearly necessary within a growing church.

Reports to the church come in several forms. The easiest to recognize, of course, is what is labeled a "report" to a World Conference. However, the evening sermons which are traditionally given during Conferences by the church's president, the president of the Quorum of Twelve, the Presiding Bishop, and the Presiding Evangelist also serve as reports of the church's progress in various areas as well as their discernment of possibilities and directions for further progress. Church leaders also report their actions and hopes for the church in other ways, particularly in articles in the *Saints Herald*, which should be studied by those who would be well prepared when they participate in a World Conference.

Delegates who do not carefully study reports before deciding how to vote on recommended legislation are remiss in their duties. Time is often taken on the conference floor by delegates asking questions and addressing issues which have been clearly answered in reports they have in hand. Most of the reports are included in the *World Conference Bulletin*, made available sufficiently in advance of the beginning of Conference for careful study. It contains such a wealth of information that it is useful for church members to register even as nonattending participants in Conference so they will receive the material for reference (as well as to receive the minutes of conference actions).

Reports are prepared in advance of each World Conference by all of the World Church quorums, standing committees, and headquarters departments under the direction of the First Presidency. Included is a great deal of information, both statistical and philosophical, about the work these groups are doing on behalf of the church. They repeatedly demonstrate how the church's leaders are taking seriously their responsibilities in accordance with church law and conference actions. They indicate how well the will of the body has been perceived and carried out. Leaders' reports typically include a description of their specific activities in the last inter-conference period in fulfilling their responsibilities, recommendations for conference actions in their areas of administrative concern, along with background information to assist the delegates in making wise judgments. They also often include strong testimonies of those leaders about the gospel and statements of their vision of the church's mission.

On many occasions, reports are also made by special committees and task forces which have been initiated either by the Presidency or by previous conference actions. Such reports typically include statistical data, opinion surveys, research into church law and previous conference actions, and usually include recommendations for further action in the area of concern. The reports furnish the background information and rationale out of which the recommended actions emerged, and from which delegates may make informed decisions.

An excellent report for review is the report on "Sources and Applications of Church Income"[7] which was given to the 1980 World Conference. This report was the summary of an extensive study by a special select committee which analyzed the financial policies of the church. Study of the report can help the delegate to understand the philosophies behind the church's budgeting and stewardship endeavors.

The seventy-eight-page report on "The Church and Higher Education"[8] which was also given to the 1980 Conference is worthy of careful study. It contains historical and philosophical overviews of the church's involvement in higher education, statistical demographic data about contemporary society and about the church's related institutions of higher learning (e.g., Graceland and Park colleges, Temple School), including a summary of financial support which the church has given them, and recommendations concerning future supportive relationships. At the 1980 Conference, delegates voted to ask for further information about a proposed closer affiliation with Park College before giving it permanent approval. The requested information was provided in a report to the 1982 World Conference which satisfied the delegates' concerns and the permanent affiliation was approved.[9] This is a good example of church administrators responding in a responsible manner to a request generated by the Conference.

The 1974 World Conference requested the First Presidency to appoint a "Task Force on Aging." The summary of the report of this task force to the 1976 Conference contains a wealth of guidance for those who want to be involved in giving ministry to, and receiving the ministry of, persons of advanced age. The entire study was made available through the church secretary, and contains extensive data to help understand the nature of the problems and opportunities related to ministries among the aging.[10]

The 1976 World Conference approved a request for a "Task Force on Single Life-Style," which was appointed by the First Presidency and gave a summary of its report to the 1978 Conference. The summary expressed well the church's commitment to ministries of "wholeness" in the single life-style. The complete study (also made available through the office of the church secretary) furnishes a great deal of data about single life-styles and information about available forms of ministry among singles.[11]

An extensive report was given by the World Conference Organization and Procedures Committee to the 1982 World Conference.[12] It contains a description of the church's organizational structure, its current system of representation, statistical data, a description of possible methods of handling the problem of the increasing size of World Conferences, and recommended changes in representation and methods of conferring. This report should be carefully studied by any who wish to understand the rationale of current systems, and particularly before preparing legislation to propose changes for the future.

Every report, whether from a special task force or committee, or from one of the presiding quorums, or a church-related institution, should be read carefully, particularly before discussing issues or proposing legislation which might relate to the area covered by the report. The report of the Presiding Bishopric should certainly be studied before consideration of the budget for future years. Because of the connection between the church's finances and the ministries it is able to provide, every member should be interested in the report of the church's financial condition and what it means in terms of ministry. "The income of the church may be reported in terms of dollars, but it must be interpreted as a reflection of the lives of our people."[13] This understanding is repeatedly expressed in reports of the Presiding Bishopric over the years. A similar recognition of the spiritual significance of financial and administrative matters in the lives of the membership and the ministries of the church can be seen in the reports of many others with administrative responsibilities.

Reports should be studied with several factors in mind, including the following:

1. *The accountability* shown in the reports of those with administrative authority who are responsible for implementing the will of the body. In this regard, it is often useful to study the reports of one Conference in conjunction with the minutes of the previous one to see how the actions of that Conference have been implemented. In a sense, the reports of the church's headquarters and divisions and standing committees are an appendage to the First Presidency's report, as the Presidency is responsible for directing and overseeing their functions.

2. *The information* which is included about implementation of the church's programs both successes and problems. This often consists of statistical data (particularly in the Presiding Bishopric's and statisticians' reports of church membership), but also overall descriptions of the activities of the church's representatives in many areas.

3. *The analyses* which the leaders have made of the data in the report, including the successes, problem areas, and opportunities which are present. Their analyses will often include a "world view" which is not always immediately obvious to those in a given jurisdiction.

4. *The recommendations for conference action* which are often included with reports. Often the reports are accompanied by specific recommendations for legislative action arising out of the analyses they have made of the data they present in the reports.

5. *The counsel* and the interpretations of the doctrine and mission of the church. Being a prophetic church does not mean simply receiving a revelatory document from time to time. It means a continually renewing interpretation of the mind and will of God in the life situations of a given time, and involves everything the church and individuals say and do. The reports and sermons of the church's leaders help make these interpretations.

The church sees itself as responding to the continuing presence of God in the human situation. It asserts that "more light and truth" is continually understood and expressed as the church faithfully responds to God's call. The faithful are told to expect to continue to receive "line upon line, precept upon precept" (D. and C. 95:3a). It necessarily follows that understandings of God's immutable truths must grow—which actually means *change* in constructive ways—with passage of time. The specific policies and programs in the work of the church will, of course, change with time, but also the basic understandings of the nature of the church and its mission in the world must grow as well. Reports and sermons of some of the General Church leaders over the years reveal their attempts to minister to their time, but also to convert the Saints to a larger vision of the nature and mission of the church in the world.[14]

In 1862, President Joseph Smith III advised a Conference:

Another thing should be avoided by the elders; and that is, preaching so hard against the various denominations, or otherwise pulling down the doctrine of the various sects, instead of building up our own. We should preach the peaceable things of the kingdom. There should be no malice, anger, or hatred; all should be kind and affectionate one to another, exercising love and charity to all. There should be no talebearing and if we are injured, say nothing at the time, but think of it and consider whether it is worthy of our notice, and let us try and forgive them; and let us examine ourselves and see if we have done altogether right. Perhaps we also may need forgiveness ourselves, and by doing so we will not be so easily injured, but will be able to go through the world smoothly.[15]

This good advice has certainly not always been followed, but remains appropriate.

Humor has sometimes found its way into reports along with philosophy. In 1871, Elder William H. Kelly, reported that while he was sleeping one night, "some stealthy hand was kind enough to remove from my pocket the little change I had with me." The thief got so little that Brother Kelly remarked further, "What a splendid joke we get on these fellows when we travel without purse or scrip entirely, which is no rare thing for us down here."[16] What a good commentary for not becoming overly burdened with possessions!

In association with some of the tensions of the early 1920s, which were well known throughout the church, Joint Council reports to the church through the *Herald* kept the church informed, both that there were difficulties, and that the work of the church was more important than any of them. A few phrases from the 1922 report of the Joint Council (written by John Rushton) demonstrate this:

Perhaps at no time in the history of the Reorganization have critical issues accumulated in as threatening a manner as at the present time [he referred both to unsettled world conditions and internal problems within the church].... The tension which was manifested during the course of the sessions was not caused by personal feelings or of individual desires for mastery, but because it was sensed that upon this association and the outcome of the several meetings the immediate future, at least, would depend. The council was also well aware of the numbers of church members who were impressed with the importance of the situation....Whatever acerbities developed during the discussion of the many matters presented, such were never outstanding features of discussion but always were incidental to the main subject, and the brethren ever were willing to overlook and forgive any trespass upon personal feelings because of the deep sense of the importance of the work which was pressed upon them for attention...it may be said without exaggeration that there was developed a spirit of unity, mutual understanding, and personal appreciation of each other which provides a foundation for future work making for the benefiting of the church at large....It is our sincere hope...that all will rally wholeheartedly to the assistance of the cause which to each one is the biggest thing needing our attention. May it please God to clarify our vision, strengthen the faith, deepen the convictions, and widen the horizon of the church consciousness; and in the passion for the saving of souls and building up of the kingdom may all be stimulated and nerved for the coming days.[17]

An interesting pithy statement was included in the report of the Second Quorum of Seventies to the 1930 Conference:

The quorum seems to be in good working condition, but our average would be higher if some of our inactive ones could be fired up or fired out. Of course we much prefer the former, and are making every effort to encourage and help each member to do his best.[18]

The Quorum of Twelve report to the same 1930 Conference indicated an expanded understanding of the responsibility of the standing ministry and of every member for doing the missionary work of the church.

One of the noticeable features of the work of the past year has been renewed realization of the vital importance of missionary work to local effectiveness. The presidents of stakes and districts and branches have joined with us in an intensive effort to make our people conscious of moral responsibility for the spiritual well-being of their neighbors...it is the sense of this body that every member of the church commit himself by the fact of his baptism and confirmation to the responsibility of spreading the gospel among his friends and neighbors in all the world by his personal life and testimony and by the payment of tithing; and that every member of the church should therefore be encouraged to share in the total missionary task of the church to the full extent of his opportunity and ability... it is the sense of this body that missionary work should be regarded not as a separate department of church enterprise, but as one of the essential functions of every department; and that every officer and member of the church in both local and general organizations should therefore seek to impregnate his work with proper missionary significance.[19]

President F. M. Smith addressed a serious problem in his report to the 1932 Conference:

Too long have we been weakened and our efforts dissipated by the Saints listening to the carping critics, and their progress hindered by doubts stirred up by mischief makers, inordinately ambitious office seekers, and self-appointed regulators. There is happiness and progress to be found by the Saints in keeping close the commandments of God and following the leadership of those whom God has appointed.[20]

How many times the same problems must be addressed over the years!

The church found its way through its serious problems with debt during the Great Depression of the 1930s because of the openness of the leaders, who reported well to the church about the nature of the problems, helped make some tough decisions in regard to them, and worked with the members to solve them. President Smith reported to the 1932 Conference,

The whole debt of the church was not a matter of sudden development. Its growth covers the period of a decade or more, and crept steadily upon us because we had a false sense of security in that our credit remained good. Curtailment of expenses should really have begun ten years ago.... There are some perhaps who even yet are disposed to concern themselves about fixing the blame... it is far more important to find and feel our way out of the dilemma. This the councils tried to do and we are still trying....The errors of a decade can hardly be corrected in a year; but that we have made progress is apparent from observation of our financial report, for it shows that 1931 closed with a surplus of income over expenses in operating expense.... Our own difficulties, if properly faced, will doubtless be effective in turning us more definitely towards our fundamentals and objectives, in efforts to reevaluate them. And while we may be temporarily checked in putting into effect some of the practical applications of our religion...we can not but feel that in getting on safer and surer financial foundations we are but organizing for a more definite drive in the direction of Zionic conditions later. Our fundamentals remain always the same....In God we still trust, and Christianity still shines as the hope of our world.[21]

The affirmative response to the church's debt problem allowed the Presiding Bishopric to report in 1938,

Because of the splendid response of the church to the Debt Payment Plan...the report herewith, accompanied by the auditor's analysis, is to us the most interesting of those it has been our privilege to submit. The schedules and exhibits reflect the story of a people whose hearts are set upon the successful completion of a task perhaps distasteful, but certainly necessary, in the performance of which they have found the unity and peace so essential to the constructive work of the future...in our work of liquidation no properties essential to the church in its missionary and zionic program have been sold or lost.[22]

They were able to report on the church making great strides even in the face of having to overcome tremendous difficulties. Finally the Presiding Bishopric reported, "Our debt was eliminated, reserves have been set aside, and annual budgetary operations have constantly been kept within our income."[23]

President Israel A. Smith, in his address to the 1952 Conference, celebrating the centennial of the Reorganization, summarized many of the achievements of the church over that one hundred years. He both acknowledged a debt to those who have gone before and challenged the church to new efforts.

Here we are by the thousands, growing in numbers, in wisdom and spiritual power, conscious of the debt we owe to our predecessors for the safe way in which they built, and more appreciative and more mindful of the "rock of revelation" on which the church was founded. Pursuant to wisdom given as needed, every step has been taken as asked by our Lord and Master whose servants we are and in whose service we here today, and in the presence of this vast concourse, pledge our continued allegiance.... Today the Reorganized Church of Jesus Christ of Latter Day Saints proclaims the gospel of Christ to the world and invites all people to join in the work of building the kingdom of God.[24]

To the Conference of 1956, the First Presidency reported its view that

We are enlisted in a great cause: the cause of the kingdom. The enterprise is by now well launched. We have a great history. This history is not the story of what we have done, but of what God has done in and through us.... We are not here to have our way, but to find God's way that we may walk therein.[25]

An "Epistle from the Council of Twelve" in 1962 stated

We have been commissioned to channel...divine power into modern life, conditioning human relationships with celestial wisdom. It is our privilege by the grace of God to reveal his word for his world.... But what does it mean to express the gospel in the changing circumstances of modern life with its technical knowledge, industry, rapid communication, and the mingling together of many people? What does it mean to express God's Word in all cultures? What does it mean to apply the universals of the gospel to the specific and varied ethnic concepts of marriage, the family, and so on? These questions require answers.[26]

Answering these fundamental questions has continued to occupy the interest of the church.

In 1964, the First Presidency's report indicated that

the growth of the church is requiring us to apply basic principles of organization in new fields and on higher levels...it is inevitable that the search for solutions will lead us into new fields, and while we must advance with care it is clear that we must advance. We cannot function effectively as a world church with the same simple organization through which we planted the church in Iowa and Illinois and Missouri a century ago....It is of major importance that those who qualify for...leadership shall be held to faith in the Lord Jesus Christ and to loyalty to his coming kingdom. It may well be that this basic faith will sometimes be expressed in terms peculiar to our age rather than in phrases which were once new but which have long since lost their relevance. We should not be unduly concerned about this. Two things are here important. One is that the truth shall be known and believed and expressed, and the other—which derives from it—is that this truth shall be seen to be relevant to the needs...in our time and in eternity.[27]

The Quorum of Twelve report of 1966 affirmed the perception that

our changing world scene requires a church which is alert to need and girding for significant action. We know that a prophetic and apostolic church cannot be so absorbed in its own chores that it loses sight of the revolutionary milieu in which we live and must fulfill our destiny....Some principles are emerging from our increasing experience with missions abroad. A major principle is that the church must be established indigenously. Leadership by nationals is the heart of this development....It is advisable to build churches and to establish procedures in light of the cultural patterns of those nations to which we go. To overlay Americanisms upon other nations which may have even more to offer in their own culture is to cloud the essentials of faith and worship and to forfeit the contributions of diverse peoples to the total life of the church.[28]

In a joint statement of the Presidency and the Twelve entitled, "The Beckonings of the Future," affirmation was given that truth can be found in multiple settings and expressed in various ways, including in ecumenical activities. "It has always been our practice to join with other groups, both religious and secular, in promoting movements which are compatible with our vision of the kingdom. This we should continue to do."[29] This thought was continued in the 1968 Conference with the First Presidency's statement that

the Restoration can be a leaven to all Christendom. It is not at odds with Christendom as a whole. The real enemy in today's world is not other Christian communities but the wickedness and strife, alienation and despair that run rampant in the world.[30]

In his 1970 conference sermon, President W. Wallace Smith stated, "Too narrow an approach to the interpretation of the gospel of Jesus Christ will not meet the needs of the discriminating individual who sees himself as serving God through the avenue of ministering to the needs of humanity."[31] He affirmed the need for the church as a distinctive organization, prophetically implementing the gospel of Christ, but also in a cooperative relationship with the other institutions of society. This need was well stated in the instruction brought to the church in 1974 that, "You who are my disciples must be found continuing in the forefront of those organizations and movements which are recognizing the worth of persons and are committed to bringing the ministry of my Son to bear on their lives" (D. and C. 151:9).

The reports and conference sermons of the church's leaders are filled with many more examples of good "food for thought" in many more subject areas than have been mentioned in the foregoing. Many of them can be properly described only by the word *prophetic.* They are well worth studying to find where the leaders feel the church has been, where it is, and where it should be going.

Visions of how the church should implement its mission have changed over the years as the church and society have changed. But commitment of the church's leaders to the basic truths of the gospel, as reflected in their reports and sermons, has been constant. Those who feel the leadership does not have clearly thought-out goals and visions for the church should read the reports and the sermons. Those who wonder what the leaders' positions are on some of the most important matters concerning the church, and those who wonder if the testimony of the leaders is valiant, should read the reports and the sermons. The reports of church leaders need to be utilized. They are an important communications medium for informing the membership so wise decisions can be made for the future.

SUMMARY

Reports are key sources of information regarding the progress and current status of the church in its various functions. They furnish important statistical information, statements of policies and philosophies, and projections for the future to serve as the background for informed decision-making. Members should study reports carefully for the information in them before legislative sessions. Reports express church leaders' accountability to the body. They also communicate to the body the leaders' visions of how the church can act prophetically in its time.

REFERENCES

1. Church History, Vol. 5, 148-149.
2. GCR 25.
3. Church History, Vol. 5, 159.
4. Ibid., 149; GCR 361.
5. Church History, Vol. 6, 524-525.
6. Ibid.
7. 1980 WCB, 189-208.
8. 1980 WCB, separately paginated.
9. 1982 WCB, 283-285, 348.
10. 1974 WCB, 221, 269; 1976 WCB, 191-196, 225. 268.
11. 1976 WCB, 190, 191; 1978 WCB, 212-213, 278.
12. 1982 WCB, 45-100.
13. *Saints' Herald—Conference Daily Edition* (April 3-4, 1938), 9.
14. Howard Booth, "Recent Shifts in Restoration Thought," *Restoration Studies I,* 169.
15. Church History, Vol. 3, 325-326.
16. *True Latter Day Saints Herald* (1871), 18:453.
17. Report of Joint Council Meeting by Elder John Rushton, *Saints' Herald* (June 14, 1922), 561, 562.
18. *Saints' Herald—Conference Daily Edition* (April 16, 1930), 105.
19. Ibid., 41, 42.
20. *Saints' Herald—Conference Daily Edition* (April 7, 1932), 23.
21. Ibid., 21, 22.
22. *Saints' Herald—Conference Daily Edition* (April 3-4, 1938), 8.
23. *Saints' Herald—Conference Daily Edition* (1958), 8.
24. *Saints' Herald—Conference Daily Edition* (March 31, 1952), 39.
25. *Saints' Herald—Conference Daily Edition* (April 10, 1956), 66.
26. 1962 WCB, 76-77.
27. 1964 WCB, 278-279, 284.
28. 1966 WCB, 66-68.
29. Ibid., 248.
30. 1968 WCB, 223.
31. 1970 WCB 245-246.

CHAPTER 8

Budgeting

KEY CONCEPT: The church operates financially by well-defined procedures according to a budget which allocates funds to programs according to priorities in the church's mission.

"Stewardship is the response of my people to the ministry of my Son and is required alike of all those who seek to build the kingdom" (D. and C. 147:5a). This principle of stewardship responsibility permeates every level within the church, from the individual member to the branch or congregation, to the stake or district, national mission, and to the World Church.

At every level the principle of the gospel implies that spirit and element belong together.

The affirmation of the Restoration prophet is that "spirit and element, inseparably connected receiveth a fullness of joy" and that "the elements are the tabernacle of God" (Doctrine and Covenants 90:5e, f). This is an incarnational principle upon which stands the process of giving form and substance to purposes and values. It is in this light that we should administer our total stewardship of temporalities. The church budget is an orderly approach to the expression of our divinely revealed purposes through the use of our physical and economic resources.[1]

"Budgets are not a fad, but a necessity in any well organized institution. The purpose of a budget is to determine the income and how that income shall be spent, instead of running without any definite financial program."[2] Simply stated, "the budget is the financial expression of the plan to achieve the objectives and goals of the church."[3]

The budget arises out of the church's overall program for accomplishing its mission. Even though the church assumes the all-ambitious commission of Christ to go into all the world and preach the gospel to every creature, limited resources do not permit doing this in all places in all ways at the same time. Resources must, therefore, be allocated so they can be used in the most effective way possible to accomplish the tasks before the church.

The specific programs, and the processes for supporting those programs, vary due to geographic, economic, and cultural limitations and opportunities.

There is a common denominator, however—the process of involving people in setting goals, making plans, determining strategies, and implementing them. Without this process, budgeting at any level of the church is an exercise in futility. Involvement in this process, on the other hand, promises significant success in the down-to-earth relationship between purpose and finances. Indeed, this process gets it all together—*mission, ministry and money.*[4]

The church budgets need to be plans for using resources wisely for ministry—plans which have been developed through the Restoration principle of "common consent." Members need to be "adequately involved with leadership in the entire process of determining objectives for the plan of ministry," through "thinking and feeling and acting together about responsibilities shared through response to the divine will."[5] As members are involved in this process, they will "own" the plan and, through having "a piece of the action," support it better than otherwise.

The church's beliefs and its allocation of resources should be consistent. This need for consistency between budget and philosophy exists at every level in the church. "The budget should arise out of the shared needs and commonly established goals of the church."[6] It is therefore essential that each portion of the church understand its particular mission in the overall work to be able to budget in light of that mission. To put it in the vernacular, budgets allow "Put[ting] our money where our mouth is."

Priorities must be established regarding which programs and functions are essential at this time and which are less urgent. Budgeting is a primary way of expressing these priorities.

Many functions are desirable; some of these are more justifiable than others, and some are fundamental to the church's mission. It follows that available income should be applied accordingly, with the more fundamental ministries receiving priority in the allocation of funds. Functions of lower priority, but highly desirable, have next claim on budgetary support, while others may have to be deferred or eliminated.[7]

The planned use of resources helps to assure the church of continued life in those areas where it is established, so that it might keep on doing the work of the Master.[8] It is also necessary to give legal sanction for the financial operations of the church by approving budgets. Thus the responsible officers are given proper authorization for the expenditure of funds as budgeted.

Recognizing the responsibility for a deliberate stewardship over its resources, the church has established that the World Church and all its subdivisions should "follow the policy of operating on an approved financial budget."[9] The World Church has given leadership in expressing this principle in sound and deliberate approaches to its budgeting over the years. In World Conferences, procedures have been established regarding budget ceilings, instructions about the use of specific funds, etc. For example, policies utilized for the World Church in recent years include the following:

A. An Operating Reserve Fund, in sufficient amount that actual expenditures for a current year may be "out of cash on hand, rather than on the basis of anticipated income."[10]

In church finances we can only be governed by the law of averages...After all, we depend upon the free will of the people to supply the funds. We cannot coerce, neither would we want to do so. But the fact that we have no way of providing for a sure and definite amount of receipts calls for the creation year by year of a reserve fund....[11]

The principle of keeping funds on hand for one year's operations of the church generally allows for "adjustments in operating costs on an annual basis, rather than on an emergency basis," but does provide for additional withdrawals for maintaining continuity of program and ministry "in times of economic stress."[12]

B. A Budget Ceiling Policy limits an operating budget to the amount of tithes and general offering income that it is estimated the church will receive in the year preceding the year under consideration.[13] Since programs, budgets, and projected incomes all have to be planned several years in advance, it is readily apparent that church officers must have flexibility in their administration, and that an operating reserve fund is necessary.

The development of a World Church budget involves much consideration and long preparation by many persons. The steps in its development include the following:

A. The First Presidency, in accord with instructions from previous World Conferences, and with its assessment of the church's resources and opportunities for programs of ministry, develops a recommended program for the accomplishment of the mission of the church. Members of the Presidency are, of course, free to consult others and to assign to the headquarters staff specific responsibilities in regard to this work. While World Conferences pass budgets for two-year periods, the program planning in many cases must be for a number of years, even decades in advance.

B. The divisions of the Presidency's staff and the general officers of the church evaluate and make proposals for funding projects, activities, personnel, and materials to implement the program. After many discussions, recommended priorities are assigned to these various proposals.

C. All budgetary requests are then considered by a Pre-appropriations Committee, which incorporates them into composite form for presentation to the Board of Appropriations for further refinement and transmission to the World Conference.[14] (The Pre-appropriations Committee includes one representative each from the First Presidency, the Council of Twelve, the Presiding Bishopric, with assistance of the other two members of the Presiding Bishopric and such other persons as they may need from time to time.)

D. The final consideration of a budget prior to presentation to the World Conference is by the full

Board of Appropriations. This is a sizable group, until 1984 consisting of the three members of the First Presidency, all members of the Council of Twelve, the three members of the Presiding Bishopric, the president of the Quorum of High Priests, the senior president of the Council of Presidents of Seventy, and fourteen members of the Order of Bishops (elected by the Order of Bishops).[15] At the 1984 World Conference, provision was made for the delegates to elect nine additional members for four-year terms on the Board of Appropriations.[16] Any member of the church is eligible for election.[17] This board is large enough (forty-three members) to be aware of most of the interests of the church throughout the world, but so large that most of the detailed work obviously must be done before it meets. The entire process must be completed in time for publication in the *Saints Herald* so delegates can study the proposed budget before Conference convenes.

The World Conference, having final authority for World Church budget approval, must exercise its authority responsibly. Even the World Conference does not have total freedom of action. The budget of the World Church reflects financial dealings in many parts of the world, and in these dealings the church is subject to the laws of the nations in which it is established. This is particularly evident in the titling and transfer of properties, and also transfers of funds among nations. Tax laws, of course, also apply to the church's personnel in the various nations where they work, and the church must comply with these laws.

When funds have been contributed by persons or action taken by a previous Conference to designate certain monies for specific purposes, the church may have legal as well as moral obligations to use them only in the manner designated. For example, the church could not ignore its financial obligations to retired appointees, even if it were to try to use the funds for other purposes. In addition, the church must meet "fixed" obligations, such as building maintenance, insurance, taxes (not all church-related operations are tax exempt), and also any previously made debts and other commitments.

Modifications of the budget at a World Conference are possible, but need to be made with fiscal responsibility as delegates consider their relation to the overall priorities of the church's program. Modifications should not be made lightly or capriciously or on the basis of "hidden agendas," such as deleting the budgets of departments or officers with which members may be displeased.

A proper reason for changing the recommended budget is that the Conference, after deliberation, comes to a different set of overall program priorities from those used in the preliminary stages of preparation of the budget. This needs to be done only after careful consideration of the effects the modifications will have on the church's entire program over the years.

Certain programs may be desirable, and even become high priority items in the near future, but the time may not yet be "ripe" for them. Certain persons essential to their success may be needed in other ministries for a time. Key persons may need a period of training, so that, even if it were budgeted a program might have to be delayed. Many programs cannot begin or be hurried along just because a lot of money is appropriated for them. Most significant programs of ministry need a "lead time" before they can be implemented, and additional money early in the process may not help.

The work of the Board of Appropriations and of the others involved in budget preparation is long and painstaking, not easily redone, and should not be changed without careful consideration. In most cases, it would appear that the World Conference should deal primarily with overall principles and priority considerations for programs. These actions could then guide the preparation of budgets to be presented at future World Conferences.

The foregoing may seem to discourage a delegate from participating actively in the budget consideration, but this should not be the case. The World Conference does have final responsibility for budget approval, and should change it if due deliberation indicates the need.

Even if the budget is not changed in Conference, all members should make it their own "financial expression of the plan to achieve the objectives and goals of the church," by evaluating carefully how it gives substance to the purposes of the church, and furthers its mission. By participating actively in considering the budget each member can more fully identify with the church's effort to use its resources well in reaching out, and feel a part of that outreach. Each can be a real part of responding to the admonition, "Therefore, go ye into all the world, and whatsoever place ye cannot go into, ye shall send, that the testimony may go from you into all the world, unto every creature" (D. and C. 83:10a).

SUMMARY

Needs and opportunities for ministry are virtually unlimited, but the church's resources are limited, and must be budgeted carefully for their most effective use. This is true at every level of the church's organization. Potential programs of ministry should be assigned priority ranks according to the contribution they will make to the church's mission, and resources should be allocated accordingly. Budgets should be consistent with and tangible expressions of the church's commitment to its stated purposes.

REFERENCES

1. "From the First Presidency," *Saints' Herald* (April 1969), 3.
2. Presiding Bishop Benjamin R. McGuire, "Budgets," *Saints' Herald* (June 28, 1922), 599.
3. "The Presiding Bishopric's Page," *Saints Herald* (November 1972), 7.
4. Ibid.
5. Ibid.
6. Ibid.
7. "From the First Presidency," 3.
8. "Financing the Church," *Saints' Herald* (April 1972), 51.
9. WCR 1008.
10. WCR 948.
11. "Budgets," 599.
12. WCR 1146.
13. Ibid.
14. WCR 1180.
15. WCR 1082 (later replaced by WCR 1180).
16. WCR 1180.
17. "Statement by the First Presidency," 1984 WCB, 334.

CHAPTER 9
Support Functions for World Conferences

KEY CONCEPT: For World Conferences to function smoothly, months of preparation and long hours of work are required by highly organized teams of persons arranging multitudes of details of supportive services.

Each World Conference is a "happening." Usually, fifteen to twenty thousand members pour into Independence, packing the restaurants, and filling hotels, motels, and homes in the community. Many people arrive several days ahead of Conference, particularly those from distant places, to meet with church leaders and to participate in some of the many pre-conference activities. These include tours of historic sites, meetings with international leaders, the delegate and visitors reception, and others. Pre-conference activities also include meetings of a number of the church's professional and interest groups (e.g., the John Whitmer Historical Association; Restoration Trail Foundation; Outreach International; medical-dental, architects, teachers, and lawyers associations). Many of these have banquets or receptions shortly before the Conference begins. There are also educational forums, quorum meetings, and *many* informal gatherings. These occur particularly among people who may have come to know one another in various parts of the world through ministerial assignments or other traveling, and now live far apart. In many respects, the World Conference resembles a gigantic reunion.

The Auditorium is a continuous beehive of activity before and during Conference. The many small meeting rooms are tightly scheduled, with overflow into the nearby Stone Church and other locations throughout the city. The "buzz" of visiting and discussions (and the swift passing of rumors) never stops. The bustling activities continue into the evenings, with preaching services, programs, concerts, and small group meetings, followed by late-night gatherings in homes all over town.

Before a World Conference session is called to order, the conference chamber, which can seat 5,800, usually looks much like the floor of a Republican or a Democratic nominating convention, with people crowding the aisles and hustling about in every direction. But when a session is called to order, the pandemonium stops. The 2,800 delegates, and approximately the same number of spectators at most sessions, become quiet and attentive and the business begins.

The business sessions are the focus of a World Conference, because doing the necessary official business of the church is the most obvious and primary reason for having a Conference. No one truly participates who does not attend the business sessions. However, there is much more to a Conference than the business sessions, and one certainly has not participated well who does not take part in other official meetings as well. Attendance at the hearings and the delegate or quorum pre-legislative sessions is often essential for a good understanding of what is said and done in the business sessions. In addition, one can only participate *fully* in a World Conference by taking part in many of the other activities, both formal and informal, which are available.

A World Conference could be likened to a feast. The hearings, pre-legislative sessions, and other meetings are the early courses; the business sessions are the main course. But both the seasoning that gives flavor to the meal and the dessert that makes it complete are to be found in the services of worship and fellowship, and in the many programs, receptions, and opportunities for visiting which are scheduled.

A "happening" doesn't just happen, nor does a feast occur without a great deal of planning and hard work in the preparation. For a World Conference to even occur, and particularly for it to run smoothly, countless hours are required on the part of hundreds of people, beginning many months before the Conference, peaking during it, and also continuing long afterward for some.

Planning for the next World Conference actually begins immediately after the previous one. The First Presidency must promptly appoint any committees or task forces that were called for by a Conference. They also must assign to the appropriate quorums or departments any topics that were referred by the Conference. The assignment will usually include designated dates and procedures for reporting back to the First Presidency or to the next Conference.

The *detailed* planning for a World Conference begins well over a year in advance of the date selected (by the previous World Conference) for the next Conference to begin. Usually in January the First Presidency names a conference manager, and a person to chair the Credentials Committee. The other conference committee chairs are then usually selected by mid-February. The committees include:

Administration to the Sick
Baby Comfort Room
Budget Control (of the budget for the conference itself)
Building, Facilities, and Parking
Communications Media
Communion Services (supervisors of serving ministers)
Floral Decorations
Historical Tours
Housekeeping Services
Housing
Information Booth
Interpreting for the Deaf
Laurel Club
Legislative Communications
Maintenance Services
Music
Nursing and First Aid Services
Physicians and Emergency Services
Post Office
Public Information
Receptions
Registration
Translations
Ushering Services
Worship Services
Youth Activities
Youth Service Corps
Others

Many of these committees coordinate with one another in their planning. For example, the Worship Committee must obviously coordinate with the committees on floral decorations, interpreting for the deaf, music, ushering services, and others. All of them coordinate with the conference manager and with budget control, as each committee has a budget for its functioning.

World Conferences run according to a strict budget. Each Conference is expected to "stand on its own feet"—to be fully funded by registration fees and offerings. Attempts are made to keep the fees as low as practicable, in keeping with the needs of the Conference. All who participate, including those who are not delegates, should register and do their part in paying the expenses of conferences.

Administrative Tasks

The *Credentials Committee* obtains data on the membership of each jurisdiction for the year prior to the Conference and makes the necessary calculations to determine how many delegates each jurisdiction is entitled to elect. Ten months prior to the Conference, the committee sends this information to the jurisdictions, with a reminder of the proper procedures for selecting delegates. Sometime during the next eight months the jurisdictions must select their delegates and alternates, and certify them to the Credentials Committee by a date in mid-February prior to the Conference. This deadline is necessary to check the lists against the membership rolls, to communicate regarding possible errors, to arrange for registration lists, and to have the Credentials Committee report with delegate lists printed for the *Conference Bulletin*. The committee continues to function during the Conference to certify alternates if the elected delegates are unable to serve.

The *Registration Committee* also has many tasks which begin long before the Conference. About a year in advance, an estimate is made of registrants and orders placed for the registration badges. (Recent Conferences have had about 8,000 registrants.) The binders for the *Conference Bulletins* have to be ordered soon afterward. As there are many non-attending registrants, more binders are needed than badges—about 10,000 for the last few years. Announcements and registration forms have to be prepared for the *Herald* and for jurisdictions about six months in advance of the Conference.

Registrations start coming in soon after January 1 of the Conference year. From that time on, the registration personnel work steadily. As the registration forms include requests for housing, and transportation from the airport, they have to coordinate their work with the committees handling these needs. (Early registration helps them do their work well.) A typical schedule has a registration booth open at the Auditorium from 8:00 a.m. to 5:00 p.m., three days a week beginning eight weeks prior to Conference, five days a week at four weeks before, and from 8:00 a.m. to 9:00 p.m. the last week before the Conference. Persons continue to register throughout the Conference week, and lost badges need to be replaced. In a recent year, one person needed *ten* replacements, losing more than one a day during the Conference! Many others have needed as many as five replacements.

Scheduling of Facilities

The task of scheduling all the meetings and activities related to a World Conference "boggles" the mind. Even scheduling the dozens of committee gatherings during the months prior to a Conference takes careful coordination to meet committee deadlines and to avoid time conflicts among the participants. As the time approaches for the Conference to begin, the job becomes even more difficult. During the week before the Conference, meeting rooms have to have been scheduled for numerous final committee and quorum meetings, and for other gatherings. To accommodate all of these meetings, the conference manager has a record of the capacities of all of the rooms in the Auditorium, the Stone Church, and many of the other church buildings in the city, along with their capacities to serve meals and provide other amenities.

Analyzing the daily schedules in a *Conference Bulletin* can give some idea of the number of meetings and the amount of planning necessary to accommodate all of them. Most of the professional organizations and interest groups make their own arrangements for banquets and meetings, but even these must be coordinated with other conference events. Time must also be reserved in rooms capable of handling the numerous legislative hearing committees, rehearsals for services, and various discussion groups and workshops.

The first Sunday of a World Conference typically includes three Communion services at the Auditorium, and twelve to fifteen worship services which are held at nearby church facilities in Independence. Each service is planned in detail to achieve distinct purposes, to minister to those with given interests, languages or ethnic backgrounds. (For those who plan worship services in congregations throughout the church, the services at World Conferences are good models.)

The weekday activities might seem easier to schedule, but even these are complicated. Virtually every room in the Auditorium and the Stone Church is used several times each day. This includes the conference chamber, which is in use almost continuously from 7:30 a.m. to 10:30 p.m. on most days for an early morning worship, a delegate pre-legislative session, a morning business session, a noon organ recital, an afternoon business session, an evening song service, a preaching service, and a late-evening program. During the day, the housekeeping and maintenance personnel have little opportunity to service the facility, so major housekeeping is scheduled late into the night to have it ready for the next day's activities.

Scheduling of Personnel

Planning for the right people to be in the right place at the right time is an even greater task than arranging for the facilities. The schedule of the World Church leaders is unbelievably complicated, with the meetings where they participate as leaders or resource persons, the many services of worship in which they are involved, the requests for consultation with persons, and their need to consult with each other regarding the conference agenda and other matters. Simply scheduling the Joint Council and their spouses for their parts in the reception for delegates and visitors, only one of their many activities, involves a complicated sign-up list. Scheduling them for ministry in the worship services throughout the week is even more involved. Without good advance planning several would be scheduled in more than one place at a time.

Scheduling of Services

The services on the first Sunday of a World Conference are planned by the Worship Committee to offer a good variety of worship for those with various interests or needs. These include services in French, German, and Spanish; Black Ministries, Indian Ministries, and Asian Ministries services; preaching; worship with the fine arts, and others. The scheduling involves many participants, including those with specialized talents in music, drama, and other worship techniques.

Brief worship services are planned for each morning during a World Conference week. Though usually about twenty minutes in length, they require planning which is just as thorough as the longer services. In many ways, the planning for the shorter services must be more carefully done because of the brief time span allowed to include a wide variety of worship forms involving people from around the world.

The evening services of Conferences are an integral part of the program. In recent years, the president of the church has presented his sermon on Sunday evening, the Council of Twelve has presented the service on Monday evening, the Presiding Bishopric on Tuesday evening, and the presiding evangelist on Thursday. The other evenings have included major musical presentations and the ordination services for those with new calls to World Church responsibilities which are traditionally a part of each Conference.

The three Communion services held the first Sunday involve a great deal of interesting planning of multitudinous details: the order of service, those who will be taking part, ushering arrangements, servers of the Communion, music, obtaining the emblems and the cups and plates, public address system, and many more.

About a year in advance 25,000 disposable Communion cups are ordered. Shortly thereafter, letters are written to several stakes asking for women's departments to prepare the Communion wine. About 120 quarts are required. They are requested to prepare it by the same recipe, as follows:

1. Wash and stem ripe Concord grapes.
2. Crush fruit and heat until fruit is soft (140°-145° if using a thermometer).
3. Strain and squeeze through 3 or 4 thicknesses of cheesecloth that has been washed and rinsed.
4. Let juice stand 6 to 8 hours or overnight (some settling will occur).
5. Carefully pour off clear juice, add 1/2 cup sugar for each quart juice, mix well. Heat in upper part of double boiler to steaming hot (170°).
6. Pour juice in hot, sterilized quart jars. Process 20 minutes in a boiling water bath.

In addition, forty-seven loaves of whole wheat bread are needed for the Communion services which are held in both the conference chamber and the assembly room (where the service is televised). To accommodate the three services, 638 wine trays and 214 bread trays are needed. (The bread trays are rapidly cleaned and refilled between services.) Volunteer teams of five persons each clean the Communion trays after each service.

Four hundred thirty carnations are used to identify the ministers who participate in the service. Specific instructions are given regarding nearly every move they make and every step they take in the service. This includes different instruction sheets for those who serve in each of the various sections of the Auditorium. Details include being appropriately dressed and groomed, being sure that those who serve in the balcony have good eyesight to see the steps, the precise pathways they will walk and positions from which they will serve, holding the trays firmly, serving the rows from "inside out," and the signals they will follow. Serving the emblems is sufficiently complicated that a rehearsal is held the day before. The same persons serve at all three services. By such careful advance preparation for the mechanics of the services, they can be performed without drawing undue attention and can contribute to the spiritual experience of those who attend.

Volunteer Services

Some of the committees are chaired by full-time World Church personnel, but several are chaired by volunteers. Most members of the planning committees are volunteers, who freely give of their expertise and time. During Conference week, hundreds work to help it run smoothly. The efforts of these volunteers should be appreciated by the many who benefit from them, but such is not always the case. Parking lot attendants, ushers, information booth volunteers, first-aid room workers and others too often have to put up with discourtesies and anger of those who make unreasonable demands. Fortunately these people are a very small minority, and volunteers usually offer outstanding models of the way people can serve one another with love.

Ushers are needed by the dozens for virtually every activity scheduled during World Conference. Ushering requires knowledge about the facilities and the scheduled activities, the ability to anticipate and respond to the needs of people, willingness to arrive early for an activity and to work hard, capacity to be friendly but firm, and knowledge of how to proceed in emergencies.

A recent letter of President Smith expressing appreciation to those who ushered in a recent World Conference expresses very well their importance to a successful conference.

Managing the crowds in a large Auditorium service is an awesome task. As many times as I have seen it, I am still impressed by the effectiveness with which you ushers go about your tasks. There are people to be helped, doors to be closed, collections to be taken, seats to be vacated, lost children to be directed, forgetful people to be reminded. The needs are too diverse, and sometimes unexpected, to all be anticipated. It takes capable people on the spot who have a real sense of ministry to meet each situation in a way that enhances worship and good feeling.

The *Youth Service Corps* performs many valuable services before and during Conferences. They are mostly "behind the scenes," but they would be sorely missed if they were not there. An incomplete list of their services includes:

Assembling conference materials—Three weeks prior to the beginning of Conference, youth volunteers assemble the binders with the conference program, pre-printed reports, and informational materials.

Staffing coat and hatcheck rooms during some of the activities at the Auditorium.

Operating microphones for some of the quorum and delegate meetings.

Passing out programs, receiving offerings, and assisting with ushering at many services and programs.

Delivering *Conference Bulletins* to the six quorum gatherings each morning.

Serving as pages for the First Presidency, the conference manager, the staff of the first-aid room, and others.

Serving as assistants to photographers and television crews and others with official responsibilities.

Housing of World Conference delegates and visitors is a major cooperative function that involves the entire community near the church's headquarters. Many visitors make their own housing arrangements, but hundreds (including many who are not members of the church) open their homes to those they have never met before who are attending a Conference. This allows many to attend who might not be able to afford to otherwise, and has many other benefits as well. (Our family life has been enriched by acquaintance with the many fine folk who have stayed with us during Conferences over the years. From the other perspective, we will never forget the way we were so graciously hosted by a family who even cared for our small daughter so we could participate in more of the Conference we attended before we moved to Independence.)

The Laurel Club is a volunteer group of women and men who work the year round preparing and serving meals for organizations and church activities. They donate the proceeds to the church and the community. (Their banquets are of a quality beyond compare.) While Conference is in session, they serve about 22,000 meals—breakfast, lunch, and dinner—with about 200 workers each day. These people serve with the kind of efficiency and friendliness that goes far beyond what one could expect. Menu planning, food pricing, and scheduling the volunteer workers occupy several months of work before Conference begins.

The information booths are staffed by volunteers who know about the community, facilities, scheduled activities—almost anything anyone needs to know. They run the message center, distribute the *Bulletin,* and take care of "lost and found."

The first-aid room is staffed morning, afternoon, and evening during World Conferences by nurses, emergency medical technicians, and other volunteers who are available to handle the first aid needs of conference participants. Those with more serious health problems are transported to the nearby Independence Regional Health Center (sponsored by the church) for appropriate care. A number of church member physicians in the community donate their time to see out-of-town participants in the first aid room for medical problems which may arise while they are at Conference. Those who live in Independence take care of their health problems in the usual way with their personal physicians.

Several receptions are held before and during World Conferences. These include the Delegate and Visitors' Reception which is scheduled on the Saturday evening that Conference begins. A number of other receptions also are given with donated food and time, in conjunction with gatherings of international leaders, for ceremonies honoring persons at the Conference, and for delegates from some of the more distant jurisdictions.

Signing for the deaf is done regularly at World Conferences by dedicated volunteers who have developed skills in sign language. The deaf or mute are seated in the right front section of the Conference Chamber, and signing is done for them at all of the business sessions and most of the worship services and evening activities.

Translation services for World Conferences is a major task provided by full-time World Church personnel and by volunteers. In a manner similar to the United Nations, simultaneous translation is provided for many of the services and pre-legislative sessions, and all of the legislative sessions. These are broadcast so that those in the chamber can tune in transistor radios to the languages they understand for translation and commentary. Recent conferences have included translations into French, German, Spanish, Japanese, Dutch, Tahitian, and Korean, and at times Navajo and Haitian Creole as well. Simultaneous translation requires unusual expertise in languages. Accurate communication of the *concept* is more important than word-for-word renditions. At the same time, the translator must be listening for the next thought to be translated. If the subject under discussion or a speaker's statements apply only in a given culture, or if certain concepts are difficult to convey in the language, the translator's task is even harder. He or she must add commentary to the translation to make it more understandable for those listening. This requires an extreme expenditure of energy and concentration by those who give this valuable service.

Translation services begin long before Conference begins. The reports of the church's presiding quorums, headquarters departments, and standing committees are translated in the various languages and sent to the appropriate jurisdictions as soon as they are available. As proposed legislative items arrive in advance of Conferences, they are also translated and sent to the jurisdictions. This work accelerates as Conference approaches, and continues while Conference is in session. As quorums and delegate sessions develop legislation during Conference, and as amendments are made in legislative sessions, translators often work late into the night to make materials available the next day.

The Public Relations Commission does another

kind of important "translation" service for the church—translating the events and actions of World Conferences into communications that are as accurate and timely as possible. World Conferences are significant news events of interest to the media. The church, of course, has no direct control over coverage given by the press, but finds that providing thorough and accurate information promptly, honestly, and openly is the best policy and generally results in fair coverage. The news media in the communities near headquarters are familiar with the church and generally do a good job of reporting. The wire services and more distant newspapers and radio and television stations have less familiarity and therefore greater problems to overcome in achieving accurate coverage.

The Public Relations Commission also begins its work long before Conference opens. A "clipping service" is subscribed to which shows what is being printed in newspapers in the United States. "Media kits" are prepared which contain announcements pertaining to the Conference, a brief history of the church, short biographies of the leaders, a glossary of terms that have special meaning within the church, a description of the agenda, and some possible story ideas. These media kits (including copies of the *Conference Bulletin*) are sent to newspapers and to radio and television stations, both in the area around headquarters and to major cities and areas where the church has concentrations of members. Pictures of leaders and of the Auditorium and of conference activities are kept immediately available for the press, as well as videotapes so that television stations can do stories without having to send their own camera crews.

A press room is available for the media at World Conferences, with telephones and connections for radio and television. Members of the First Presidency (and sometimes other church leaders) are available at scheduled times for interviews with media representatives. They must be ready with an immediate response to questions, even about difficult issues. Working closely and openly with the press results in positive benefits for the church. The church benefits when what it does is thoroughly analyzed and honestly expressed, either through an individual's investigation and testimony or through good coverage by the public media.

Advance preparation is also necessary for the "dignitaries" who come to World Conferences. Typically, the Conference will be greeted by the governor of Missouri, a United States senator, or other well-known political figure, who is usually introduced by the mayor of Independence. Much advance planning is required, including transportation, security, and hosting, all worked out carefully with the guest's staff. This includes lists of exactly who will be involved, where people will be sitting and walking, and a careful agenda of precisely what is to be expected at each point in the honored guest's participation.

The secretarial work that goes into preparing for and holding a World Conference staggers the mind. The memoranda and correspondence of headquarters personnel and committees, and of individuals throughout the world involve thousands of pages of materials. During the Conference, simply having the right information at the right place at the right time—for the presider to have at hand for the proper moment in a legislative session, or for a resource person to respond to a question involves efficient systems of filing and data retrieval that are often taken for granted by those who expect the information to be available at all times.

The church secretary and staff begin some of their most intensive work when most delegates are beginning to relax after a legislative session is finished. They must immediately begin the task of writing the minutes of the day's session, reading and rereading them for accuracy. Added to the minutes are the many announcements, biographical sketches of nominees for elections, printing of new legislation, reports of hearing committees, etc. All of these materials must be assembled and checked for authenticity and accuracy in time to get them to the Herald Publishing House for printing for the next day's session. The people at the publishing house work through most of the night to have the daily *Bulletins* ready for the next morning's sessions.

Herald Publishing House, of course, does most of its work for the church continually, not just World Conference materials. But it helps in regard to Conferences in numerous ways. It publishes the *Saints Herald*, the church's official magazine for publication of notices, reports, etc. Articles are solicited from the church's leaders and others to inform about contemporary issues, actions, and counsel of leadership, how Conferences work, etc. "Human interest" stories help members appreciate the preparations many are making for an effective and interesting Conference. The articles in the *Herald* after Conference are also helpful for understanding what happened.

Conference Bulletin is a remarkable and useful book—the result of the combined effort of many people. It is a valuable resource for communication before, during, and after a World Conference—the most valuable single resource to understand what is *going* to happen, what *is* happening, and what *did* happen at a given Conference. The *Bulletin,* of course, includes the daily schedule of what is happening when and where. It also contains emergency and safety information, the location of first-aid and other special services, seating plans, locations of offices, a selection of hymns which will be used in the Conference, a synopsis of parliamentary procedure, and some simple rules for courteous and effective participation in the Conference. Most of the questions asked at the information desk have answers already available in the *Bulletin.*

Also in the *Bulletin* are the reports of World Church councils and quorums, the headquarters divisions, the standing committees and task forces, and the church-related institutions.

After a World Conference, the *Bulletin* serves as a valuable reference. The reports contain information useful for understanding where the church stands in its kingdom-building enterprises. The minutes give a more complete story than just summarizing the final legislative actions. Study of a series of *Bulletins* over a period of years gives an even more complete story—leading to an appreciation of the immense amount of work which goes into developing them. Noting all the activities announced and described in the *Conference Bulletin,* and the work that goes into preparing for and making them succeed, one can begin to perceive how much work goes into making World Conference a good experience.

The foregoing gives only a slight taste of the extreme devotion of those who expend so much effort to make a World Conference succeed in doing the work of the church. Many who are employed by the church go far beyond the "call of duty" to make the experience of conference participants comfortable, safe, enjoyable, and effective. Many others volunteer their time and energy; each Conference provides countless examples of people serving others in selfless Christian love. Everyone who benefits, i.e., the entire church, should appreciate those who work so hard for members to do the church's business and have such rewarding spiritual experiences in the process.

SUMMARY

The success of World Conferences depends on the careful preparation and devoted service of many persons. It requires freely given expertise and long hours, both by those who are employed by the church and by hosts of volunteers. All who participate in a Conference should appreciate the contribution to their safety, comfort, enjoyment, and their opportunity to benefit from the experience due to the selfless efforts of these persons.

REFERENCES

The material for this chapter was obtained largely from two three-inch-thick notebooks maintained by the World Conference manager to work from in coordinating the thousands of tasks required to successfully organize and manage a Conference. Other material was obtained by personal interviews with committee chairpersons and members of committees. A great part was obtained simply by personal observation of the many Conferences we have attended.

CHAPTER 10
The Legislative Process—Ideals and Philosophy

KEY CONCEPT: The idea of conferring openly and reaching consensus should be kept in mind to be achieved as closely as possible in the legislative process.

As a church we believe that God is at work in the world, bringing to pass divine purposes. Because it is the work and glory of God "to bring to pass the immortality and eternal life of man," including all persons, the church doing God's work "must comprehend in some measure the meaning of that phrase and find ways to implement the program which has such a goal as its ultimate objective. We are called to wrestle with the central issues of our time."[1] This requires prophetic leadership of a people who also experience pervasive inspiration as they are involved in the processes of achieving common consent.

"Those who exercise common consent think and feel together about responsibilities which they share."[2] They will be more interested in "the process of achieving mutual understanding rather than merely getting a majority vote,"[3] though voting is necessary in legislative sessions as large as World Conferences. The church must remain true to its ideals, affirming the worth of every person in its processes of decision-making, as well as in the substance of the decisions which are made.

These understandings lay several responsibilities on the participants in Conferences and on the jurisdictions which select delegates and submit proposed legislation to the World Conference.

Individual members who would most effectively participate in a World Conference demonstrating the principles of Christ in its legislative processes will do the following:

- Appreciate and respect the individuality, worth, and rights of all other participants, and have a basic trust of their good will and motivation, whether or not they agree on specific issues.
- Prepare well for the legislative process by doing the following: learning the procedures by which Conferences function, and studying pre-conference reports, previous conference minutes, proposed legislation, and other materials available.
- Attend all legislative sessions and appropriate quorum or delegate sessions where information is received and conferring occurs.
- Listen to all discussions carefully; attempt to understand the concerns and viewpoints of all who speak.
- Participate by speaking, contributing information or viewpoints which should be considered.
- Make motions solely for the purpose of furthering the benefit and deliberate will of the body.
- Vote with regard to what will further the mission of the church and be a unifying force within the body.

- Prepare to report back to home jurisdictions about the actions and events of the Conference.
- Have a prayerful attitude.

Jurisdictions that most fully support the World Church in the tasks which are laid upon all will do the following:

- Select responsible delegates to World Conferences who represent a balance of the backgrounds and viewpoints within the jurisdiction and who will prepare for being good delegates and will participate responsibly.
- Submit legislation to the World Conference which is of general concern rather than of parochial interest, and which furthers the mission of the church.
- Assist their delegates in preparation by providing means prior to the World Conference whereby they can be informed as to how Conferences are organized and function, receive reports, proposed legislation, and other materials, and hear the viewpoints and concerns of people in their jurisdiction and engage in the process of conferring.
- Help their delegates to attend the World Conference by assistance in "covering" their responsibilities at home and at work when possible. They may also give financial assistance when needed by delegates to help defray the costs of attending the Conference.
- Trust their delegates to exercise their agency responsibly on behalf of the jurisdiction and the entire church.
- Arrange to receive reports from their delegates after the Conference so the significance of the actions of the World Conference can be interpreted for their jurisdiction.

Though these ideal characteristics of responsible jurisdictions and delegates may seem to be unattainable this is not the case. Just such devotion to the principles of common consent and the mission of the church has been observed among people at many Conferences over the years. Good will and good intent are usually present in abundance at World Conferences. These attributes, however, are not sufficient; individuals must communicate well with one another if they are to come to a unified corporate expression of devotion to God's work. If they capture the urgency and purpose of reasoning together, they will have the sense and benefit of God's promise as stated by Isaiah in another time:

Cease to do evil; Learn to do well; seek judgment, relieve the oppressed, judge the fatherless, plead for the widow. Come now, and let us reason together, saith the Lord; though your sins be as scarlet, they shall be as white as snow; though they be red like crimson, they shall be as wool. If ye be willing and obedient, ye shall eat the good of the land...afterward thou shalt be called, The city of righteousness, the faithful city. Zion shall be redeemed with judgment, and her converts with righteousness.—Isaiah 1:16-19, 26-27

Reasoning together, however, is not always easy, even among persons of good will. Failure to know *how* to reason together is more often the problem in achieving common consent than is lack of desire or good will, or even difference of opinions. Effective reasoning together is a deliberate process that takes careful planning and structuring. Conferences should be structured to *enable* the processes of reasoning together. This is provided for in several ways.

In the weeks and months before Conference, participants are given information well in advance so that they may make intelligent preparation. This includes publication of reports and proposed legislation as it becomes available, primarily in the *Saints*

132

Herald. Prior to Conference the *Herald* usually contains articles and editorials that orient people to philosophies, issues, and methods in conferring. All of this helps participants prepare for Conference, in both knowledge and attitude.

Within the limitations of time and facilities, those who organize Conference attempt to provide significant opportunity for conferring and receiving information outside the actual legislative sessions. This includes scheduled meetings of the quorums (usually starting before the week of World Conference), meetings of the Aaronic and Melchisedec priesthood, and delegate and visitors' sessions. The subjects of the "pre-legislative" sessions are geared as much as possible to the upcoming agenda of the legislative sessions, and resource persons are present to provide information and participate in discussions with the members of the Conference.

Hearing committees have become a significant part of World Conferences the last several years, and their role is expanding. Hearings begin on the Saturday morning before Conference actually convenes and are held concerning all legislation except for some of the simplest "housekeeping" items. Proposed legislation is discussed, not debated, in the hearings. Conferring in these sessions often clarifies issues sufficiently to avoid the loss of time in debating them later in the legislative sessions.

Pre-legislative sessions successfully enhance the work of the legislative sessions only insofar as persons attend and participate in them. Those who do not do this will often occupy time in legislative sessions with discussion of points which have already been satisfactorily covered for others in the pre-legislative sessions. Each member of the Conference is responsible to the body for the best use of its time—this includes participation in the conferring process prior to legislative sessions.

Conferring is possible in legislative sessions, but only to a limited extent, and if the members are sufficiently intent on it. These sessions function according to parliamentary procedure,[4] which is more geared to debating than conferring. Under parliamentary procedure, each member who can "get the floor" on an issue has only one turn to advocate a position or to make a motion until after all others who wish to speak have had a turn. The opportunity for an exchange of ideas is limited, as are the number of options one can consider in casting a vote. In spite of its limitations, parliamentary procedure may be the best method yet devised to enable assemblies of any size, with due regard for every member's opinion, to arrive at the general will on a maximum number of questions of varying complexities in a minimum time and under all kinds of internal climate—ranging from total harmony to hardened or impassioned division of opinion. An analysis of the principles of parliamentary law will show that they are constructed with careful regard for the rights of the majority to rule, the rights of the minority to be heard, and the rights of individual members within the assembly to participate.[5]

The "general will," in this sense, does not always imply even near unanimity or "consensus," but rather the right of the *deliberate* majority to decide. Complementary to this right is the right of the minority—at least a strong minority—to require the majority to be *deliberate*—that is, to act according to its considered judgment after a full and fair "working through" of the issues involved.[6]

As has been stated in Chapter 4, the majority has no right to expect the minority to support its decision unless the minority's viewpoint has been seriously taken into consideration before the decision.

A great contribution of parliamentary procedure is

that majority decisions can be made even in the presence of a great division of opinion, thus allowing the body to proceed with its work rather than to be paralyzed.

For parliamentary procedure to make its proper contribution to constructive and democratic meetings, it should be followed from the beginning as a matter of course, and should not be regarded as something to be resorted to only when trouble arises. At the same time, there should always be a flexibility as to the strictness of application of the rules—dependent on the particular situation and the members' knowledge of parliamentary procedure. Under no circumstances should concern for parliamentary correctness be permitted to impose undue artificiality in a business meeting.[7]

The great purpose of all rules and forms is to subserve the will of the assembly rather than to restrain it; to facilitate, and not to obstruct, the expression of their deliberative sense.[8]

These excerpts from *Robert's Rules of Order* make it plain that the rules exist for the benefit of the body, not vice versa. Rules should be followed with the flexibility necessary to facilitate what is actually the will of the body. As a practical matter, this means respecting the right of the First Presidency in World Conference (and of other lawful presiders in other deliberative assemblies) to vary from strict adherence to parliamentary procedure when it will, in their opinion, better serve the interests of the church. The body, of course, has the final say in demanding strict adherence, but in most cases this would defeat its own purposes. In such situations, members would do well to ask themselves if they are truly following the admonition that "all things shall be done by common consent in the church, by much prayer and faith" (D. and C. 25:1b). "Methods of reaching a decision should unite the group and generate cooperation rather than be divisive."[9]

Decision making is a complex process...Its complexity is multiplied when persons from widely varying settings and cultures endeavor to make group decisions which commit members of the World Church to certain actions or responsibilities. Faith in God, supplication through mighty prayer, trust in divinely chosen leadership, and confidence in the will of the people who are members of the World Conference should be inherent in the decision-making process.[10]

Each member should recognize his or her position as a part of the "great and marvelous work" of God spanning the centuries and the continents, and not get caught up in trivialities or momentary and parochial concerns. Each should be aware

that institutions and nations and peoples have a continuing life beyond the existence of any individual. Hence the church has a corporate life and authority which is bigger than we are and in a sense we are subsumed into it, but we can never place the institution above the worth of human personality nor believe that the church exists for any objective higher than bringing to pass the immortality and eternal life of man.[11]

The loftiest decisions are useless if in the process human dignity is destroyed and love diminished. All that is done in the World Conference should affirm the worth of all peoples, their agency, and their group responsibilities in relation to the will of God. With mutual agreement, under God, we can fulfill the dream of the ages—"That universal and peaceable kingdom which has not yet been fully realized in its glorious entirety, but is already in the process of becoming."[12]

SUMMARY

To be the body of Christ, the church must express its ideals about the worth of all persons in its processes of decision making as well as in the substance of the decisions which are made. This requires careful selection of delegates and preparation and participation by delegates, and knowledgeable and respectful sharing in conferring and legislative sessions. Structured procedures are necessary for the legislative sessions, but the structures should serve the needs of the body rather than being allowed to rule it. It is possible to come together with good will, good intent, efficiency, and competence and legislate within the church to further God's mission.

REFERENCES

1. Clifford Cole, "Prophetic Leadership," *Saints Herald* (Nov. 1972), 11.
2. Robert Bruch, "The Decision-Making Process," *Saints Herald* (February 1976), 35.
3. Ibid.
4. WCR 1156.
5. "Decision-Making Process," Bruch, 36.
6. *Robert's Rules of Order Revised,* Morrow and Company, Inc. (1971) Foreword, iii.
7. Ibid., vi.
8. Ibid., 242.
9. "Decision-Making Process," Bruch, 36.
10. Ibid.
11. "Prophetic Leadership," Cole, 11.
12. "Decision-Making Process," Bruch, 36.

CHAPTER 11

Preparation and Introduction of Legislation

KEY CONCEPT: In order to be effective, legislation must be clearly and constructively written, appropriate to the mission of the church, and presented according to well-defined methods for consideration.

"Let the words of my mouth, and the meditation of my heart, be acceptable in thy sight, O Lord, my strength, and my redeemer" (Psalm 19:14). These words of the psalmist, often used as a benediction in a worship service, would well be remembered by all who write legislation or speak in Conference.

Those who see the church as being involved with God in "a marvelous work" that spans the length and breadth of human history will not occupy the time and attention of the body with trivialities, but only with significant contributions to the work. Large or small, all items for legislative consideration should be evaluated according to whether or not they further the mission of the church.

Prayerful meditation and study concerning the church and God's mission are required to develop the judgment to know the difference between trivial and significant contributions. Judgment is also needed to decide whether an issue should be submitted for legislative action or if there are other ways to achieve a desirable goal. Only when it appears that the mission of the church can be furthered best by means of legislative action should this be called for in the legislative assembly. All legislation submitted to a World Conference should be of general interest and contribute to stating and implementing the church's mission.

Effective and constructive legislation in Conference is impossible in a number of areas:

Policies of institutions with boards of trustees cannot legally be legislated within Conferences. Such institutions as Graceland College, Park College, the Independence Regional Health Center, and Herald House are church-related, but are legally separate from the church. They have boards of trustees which are responsible for, and must be allowed to exercise, trusteeship according to the laws of the land. The interests of the church in these institutions are safeguarded by the church's approval of their articles of incorporation in some cases (Appendices E & F of *Rules and Resolutions*), but primarily by the power of the World Conferences to select or sustain most of the persons who serve on such boards. Other legislative action regarding the functioning of these institutions is limited to advising their boards of the thoughts or desires of the Conference in regard to the actions they take.

Program details in the operation of the church are beyond the time or competence of World Conferences to handle. The details of program planning, implementation, and resource development are a full-time continuing process for which the Conference legislates general policy guidelines. Implementation of programs and resource production involve employing persons with professional and vocational skills in given areas. These persons work under the administrative direction of the First Presidency, in response to needs and opportunities which become known from the fields of ministry throughout the church.

Administrative details in the day-to-day operations of the church are beyond the capability or prerogatives of the Conference to handle. These are assigned under church law[1] to the First Presidency, with others to assist them in appropriate circumstances. The legislative body has no appropriate role in, for example, setting an individual appointee's family living allowance, assigning specific duties among the executive staff, or editing specific resource materials, or involving itself in the many administrative decisions which must be made. Also, World Conferences assemble at relatively infrequent intervals. In today's world, events occur and situations change so rapidly that the administrative staff must be free to adapt appropriately, within the general policies established by Conferences.

Judicial matters, requiring confidentiality and weighing of evidence and application of church law, are impossible for Conferences to handle, and by the laws of the church are taken care of elsewhere.[2]

Individual morality which is unenforceable is not amenable to effective legislation, except in very limited ways. Through the years the church has struggled repeatedly with attempts to legislate standards of conduct and has made some statements for the guidance of members. These have sometimes been helpful and have sometimes created misunderstanding rather than clarification. When statements are made, they need to reflect the worldwide nature of the church and an understanding of their possible meanings in different cultures, for example, the symbolic meaning of dancing to different peoples. This is obvious in a piece of legislation which states

That the world fellowship of the Saints, encompassing cultures where different sets of values prevail in respect to the same or similar activities, involving factors sometimes beyond the scope of knowledge and experience of persons not in the same culture, requires the Saints to refrain from passing unrighteous judgment on the conduct of members of the church in other cultures, while each one brings his own life under discipline according to the doctrine of the church and through response to the Holy Spirit.[3]

Just because something is important (and the importance of personal morality is not questioned) does not mean it can be effectively legislated into being. Too much legislation in this regard can "make a man an offender for a word" (Isa. 29:31), and make it more difficult to draw persons into the circle of fellowship within the church.

Doctrinal statements, while they can be made in legislation, are usually ineffectual, because they cannot be binding on individual conscience, and have to be interpreted themselves. The body cannot legislate nor effectively monitor what an individual member believes. Items which can be legislated are practices of the body in relation to doctrines, such as in WCR 212 describing baptisms by immersion. Most matters in this regard would best be left, however, to the responsibility of the church's administrators for their proper interpretation and enforcement. The church has long taken justifiable pride that it has no fixed creed. A favorite hymn of the Saints begins, "We limit not the truth of God to our poor reach of mind," and ends, "The Lord hath yet more light and truth to break forth from his word."[4] Fixed doctrinal statements will usually be "partial and confined" "by notions of our day," and if the statements are not perfect may tend to hold the body back from receiving more light and truth as readily as it should.

Resolutions with hidden meanings or purposes have no place on the Conference floor. The body, including every segment within it, has the right to understand the meaning and implications of every legislative statement it considers. If committees are dissolved, if previous legislation is rescinded, if actions will be required of individuals or groups, these should be made clear within the resolution and the associated discussion. The full implications of a resolution should be as clear as possible before the body makes a decision. Probably the most frequent and serious "hidden meaning" in many resolutions is an implied or stated censure in the preamble which would indicate that some individual or group is felt to have been derelict in some duties on behalf of the body. Censure (and even lesser criticism of persons) is a serious matter. If it were ever appropriate in a legislative session, it would be only in a forthright manner and with clear meaning. It is better handled, however, outside of legislative sesions.

Effective and constructive legislation is possible in many areas apart from the limitations which have been mentioned. It is, of course, necessary at every World Conference to legislate a budget for the church. In addition, legislation establishing worthwhile programs of ministry has been introduced by jurisdictions, quorums, and committees, and by individual members who have perceived opportunities for the church to fulfill its mission.

Proper resolutions are almost always characterized by their affirmative nature. Expressions of being *against* something very rarely can further the mission of the church as effectively as expressions of being *for*. Even if one's position involves opposition to others' positions or actions, it is usually more constructive and unifying to state legislation affirmatively. Affirmative legislation arising from within the body has assisted the church in the past in many ways, including instituting programs of ministry, setting administrative policies and program emphases, calling for studies and clarification of doctrines and practices, and affirming positions of the church in relationship to world issues.

Effective legislation is logical, straightforward, and unambiguous. It usually consists of two parts, a preamble and enacting clause or clauses. The preamble usually starts with "Whereas" and states assumptions *why* something should be done. The enacting section starts with "Be it resolved," and states *what* is to be done.

The preamble is a statement of understandings out of which the legislation arises. If the reasons are obvious, a preamble is not needed. The preamble is not binding on the body, but if accepted must be regarded as stating its feelings. The statements in a preamble are therefore important and should be carefully written. If the preamble is lengthy and involved, the logic for the resolved action may be weak and circuitous, or the writers may want to have a "hidden agenda" in the preamble accepted as much as to have the "resolved" enacted. A lengthy preamble giving many reasons for an action may interfere with its chance of acceptance by the body. Even if the members agree with the resolved action, they may vote against passage because they disagree with the preamble. The best preamble, therefore, is logical, straightforward, and relatively brief.

Enacting clauses should state the resolved action succinctly and logically. They should be consistent with church law and doctrine, reasonable, and possible of attainment by those expected to implement the will of the body. Resolutions which cannot reasonably be implemented are just as much out of order as those which are in actual conflict with church law.

It is critical that those individuals who prepare legislation for submission to World Conference keep in clear focus that the subject matter must be appropriate and the writing of high quality for it to be adopted. Good ideas are just the beginning. The way the ideas are presented in the resolution is essential to final adoption. Individuals should work with one another to refine resolutions to their best form before presenting them to a jurisdictional conference, committee, quorum, or caucus meeting. These bodies can do only a limited amount of conferring and refinement of legislation, but can do much more if the original work is of good quality. By the time legislation reaches the World Conference floor, there is no longer much opportunity for refinement. Parliamentary procedure and time limitations allow for only a limited number of options to be considered. A good idea may fail to be accepted because the resolution was never sufficiently refined to express it adequately.

Legislation may be introduced to the World Conference from several different sources:[5]

1. By passage at a prior conference in a region, stake, metropole, district, national church, or tribal church, or in a branch not in one of these jurisdictions.

2. By passage within any of the World Church quorums, orders, or councils, or standing committees of the Conference, in meetings either prior to or at the time of World Conference.

3. By passage at the mass meetings of the elders or of the Aaronic priesthood held in conjunction with the World Conference, or at the meetings of "a delegate caucus composed of all elected delegates who are not members of quorums, councils, orders, or committees of World Conference." Legislation to be submitted from the mass meetings must receive a majority vote of the delegates in the meetings.[6] Delegate caucuses require at least 200 delegates to be convened, and consider agenda items which have at least 50 delegate signatures. By a majority vote they can then forward items for consideration.[7]

A number of different resolutions often are submitted from various sources (e.g., a number of different jurisdictions) concerning the same general subject. Obviously they cannot all be adopted. The quorums, mass meetings, and delegate caucus can confer during Conference to evaluate the best response to the various resolutions. Often the best response is to develop other legislation which combines or otherwise handles the concerns expressed in the resolutions or discussions brought forth at the Conference. This is one of the most significant ways that conferring assists the legislative process.

Proposals to amend the basic *Rules of Order* of the World Church must be submitted in time to be published in the *Saints Herald* at least sixty days prior to the World Conference.[8]

All legislative proposals which have been introduced into the World Conference by any of the appropriate routes are assigned by the First Presidency to hearing committees, "to facilitate consideration, consolidation, and disposition of all resolutions submitted to the World Conference."[9] The First Presidency is designated by the Conference to establish the specific rules, procedures, and membership of the hearing committees.

Hearings are structured for informing and discussing, not debating. Two hours are usually devoted to hearing each proposal. If multiple resolutions are nearly identical, they may be grouped together for one hearing—otherwise each piece of proposed legislation receives a separate hearing. Proponents of the legislation have the opportunity to explain why they think it should be adopted, and a World Church representative describes the effect the legislation may have on the church's programs and policies. Delegates may then ask questions of the resource persons and make comments for clarification as well. Following the hearing, the members of the committee are responsible for briefly summarizing the discussion in a report to the Conference as a whole.

Hearing committees do not prevent consideration of the legislation by the Conference, but give opportunity for more thorough discussion than is possible in the legislative sessions. Therefore, delegates should attend and participate in the hearings for the clarification they can receive. This may prevent needless questions and comments during the legislative sessions.

Legislative proposals which have been properly submitted, and have gone through the hearing committee process, will be called to the Conference floor by the presiders at what they consider to be the appropriate point in the agenda. If a delegate wishes to modify the agenda, this may be done by motion and vote of the World Conference. When legislation is called to the attention of the body by the presider, opportunity is given for a delegate to move its adoption and for another to second. Unless someone objects to its consideration or it is ruled out of order, the legislation is brought before the body by the presider, after which it is ready to be handled according to proper parliamentary procedure.

SUMMARY

Good legislation begins from an attitude of prayerful devotion to that which furthers God's work in the programs of the church. It should be affirmative, clearly written, straightforward, consistent with church law, and possible to implement. Legislation may come to the World Conference from jurisdictions of the church, or from the various quorums, councils, orders, committees, mass meetings, and the delegate caucus. All of these groups meet during the Conference and can confer and refine legislation introduced by their members.

REFERENCES

1. Rules of Order II:10.
2. Ibid., II:14.
3. WCR 1085.
4. *Hymns of the Saints,* No. 309.
5. WCR 1169.
6. WCR 1125.
7. Report of the Conference Organization and Procedures Committee, 1984 WCB, p. 233.
8. Rules of Order X.
9. WCR 1168.

CHAPTER 12
Parliamentary Procedure

KEY CONCEPT: Parliamentary procedure is followed to assist the body to confer in an orderly fashion and to ensure that decisions of the body represent the will of a deliberate majority. To be effective, parliamentary procedure must be understood and used constructively by the members of the body.

The term *parliamentary procedure* or *parliamentary law* originally referred to the rules and customs used for carrying on business in the British Parliament.[1] These rules and customs developed through a growing process of decisions and precedents, stating ways that were found to assist the Parliament do business effectively.

Many people have written manuals of parliamentary procedure for the use of deliberative assemblies. The best known is *Robert's Rules of Order* written by General Henry M. Robert in response to a need—"Without warning, he was asked to preside over a meeting, and did not know how."[2] He stated that at that time he "plunged in, trusting to Providence that the assembly would behave itself,"[3] but he determined that never again would he attend a meeting without knowing parliamentary law. His basic guide was first published in 1876, and has undergone many revisions. It was "based, in its general principles, upon the rules and practice of Congress, and adapted in its details, to the use of ordinary societies."[4]

Robert saw his *Rules of Order* as a guide for any organization to use, but wrote that organizations should modify and adapt them to their special situations.[5] He recognized that the corporate charter of an incorporated organization supersedes all its other rules,[6] and that next in order of precedence come the organization's bylaws and standing rules of order. For the church, these may be found in the book, *Rules and Resolutions,* which should be studied and utilized by all those who participate in World Conferences and business meetings in the church.

Following in precedence, and supplementary to the organization's charter (where it is incorporated), and to the bylaws and rules of order, are general guides such as *Robert's Rules of Order.* In 1970, the World Conference adopted a resolution "That *Robert's Rules of Order* be followed as a guide for parliamentary procedure in conducting the business of the church at all levels."[7] The traditions of parliamentary procedure, as well as the contents of *Robert's Rules of Order* are not universally known, practiced, and respected in all of the nations where the church is established. The procedures which have been adopted have come out of the cultural and historical roots of an Anglo-Saxon tradition to which many delegates are unaccustomed. In 1980, due to the recognition that not all of the world knew about and lived by *Robert's Rules of Order,* this policy was modified to apply only to those parts of the world familiar with it.[8] Inasmuch as the World Conference is an international body, further adaptations in methods of doing business will almost certainly be required for the church to more closely achieve the ideals of common consent.

Whatever rules of parliamentary procedure are ultimately utilized, they should be based on the concerns expressed in *Robert's Rules of Order*—that they be seen to be constructed upon a careful balance of the rights of persons or of subgroups within an organization's or an assembly's total membership. That is, these rules are based on a regard for the rights
—of the majority,
—of the minority, especially a strong minority—greater than one third,
—of individual members,
—of absentees, and
—of all these together.[9]

These principles should be kept in mind continually, both when procedures are established for the body to follow and by presiders and other participants engaging in the parliamentary process.

Parliamentary procedure begins with certain formalities to get the body properly organized and the deliberations under way. These should not be thought of as "mere" formalities, because they have a legal as well as symbolic significance. Without them, serious doubt could be raised as to the legality of the conference actions which would follow. With them, the Conference begins on a sound footing in doing the business of the church.

The presider begins the meeting by calling the assembly to order at the appointed time, which has been set either by previous conference action or according to the provisions of the Rules of Order. The next order of business is for the Conference to formally select the presider. In a World Conference, this is normally the First Presidency, but in its absence or disqualification the Council of Twelve would so function.[10] In the various jurisdictions of the church, presiding is by the appropriate jurisdictional presidency, or on occasion by an appropriate higher jurisdictional officer, such as a member of the First Presidency or a member of the Council of Twelve.[11]

After the selection of the presider in a delegate conference (such as a World Conference) comes the report of the credentials committee, which names those who have proper credentials, and establishes their right to act as members of the Conference on behalf of the church.

By custom, the First Presidency, having an overall view of the business to be done, presents an agenda which will in its opinion be efficient and logical. Because of time considerations, new business and prior actions in the Conference, some flexibility must be allowed in following this agenda. The Conference can vote, of course, to make its own agenda or to take an item out of the announced order, but this is rarely appropriate. As mentioned in chapter 10, those who preside should have the flexibility necessary to facilitate the will of the body as opposed to strict adherence to a set of rules.

The formalities having been accomplished, the agenda is then taken up as indicated. The agenda usually follows certain principles, which have actually been spelled out for districts and branch business meetings.[12] This includes the consideration and approval of minutes from the last previous session of the body, then the receipt and approval of any appropriate reports of officers, administrative groups or committees, quorums, or other. After this comes consideration of any old business carried over from prior sessions, followed by new business.[13]

In World Conferences, most items of business have been previously published. At the time considered appropriate, the presider calls the item to the attention of the Conference and (unless it is ruled out of order by the presider) will give opportunity for a member of the Conference to obtain the floor and move its adoption. Sometimes, opportunity to move adoption will be given to a delegate known to have introduced the resolution, or to the leader of the group which forwarded it to the World Conference.

Most main motions require a second, so at this point opportunity is given for another member to second the motion. (Items which have been presented by boards or committees do not require seconds, as their presentation to the assembly implies the support of more than one member.)[14] While it is not a legal requirement that the seconder formally obtain the floor,[15] in a large assembly this is usually done.

The role of a seconder is not always understood. "A second merely implies that the seconder agrees that the motion should *come before the meeting*," and not necessarily that the seconder favors the motion.[16] The seconder even may wish to see the assembly go on record as rejecting the proposal, after having debated it.

A motion moved and seconded without objection is then restated by the presider, or described and summarized if it is lengthy.[17] At this point it is properly before the body for discussion and disposition in one of several ways.

Discussion is a better term for the consideration of motions in church assemblies than *debate*. It is much more appropriate to the admonition, "Come now, and let us reason together" (Isa. 1:18), and to modern scriptural counsel to do all things by the principle of common consent. Nevertheless, occasions occur, even among like-minded people with regard to ultimate goals, when opinions are quite diverse about immediate actions before the body. In these situations it is essential that the debate that occurs be directed at the issues and concerns rather than at personalities. Respect should be maintained at all times for the integrity and worth of all other persons as the issues are considered.

In the discussion of a motion, the one who moved adoption of the motion has the right to the floor for the first opportunity to speak.[18] No such right is reserved for the seconder, and the right is not transferable.[19] After the mover of a motion has been accorded the opportunity to speak, all others must obtain the floor in proper fashion in order to speak.

Since 1982 the procedure for obtaining the floor in World Conferences has been different from that in other assemblies. A computerized system was introduced to assist in the process. The delegate goes to a station in the Conference Chamber where an attendant receives the delegate's registration number for entry into the computer, along with designation of the way the delegate wishes to participate—to speak for or against the motion on the floor, make another appropriate motion, or other action. The presider can then see on a computerized display the list of those who want to speak. From this point, the principles of participation are the same as in other assemblies.

In assemblies without computerization, the proper way to obtain the floor is for the member, *after the previous speaker has yielded the floor*, to stand and address the presider with the appropriate title, for example, "Mr. President." Standing before the previous speaker yields the floor, or standing without addressing the presider brings no right of recognition to obtain the floor.[20]

If opinion is divided on an issue, the presider "should attempt to give the floor to first a proponent and then an opponent. It is not always possible to know who will speak for and who against, but as far as is possible this should be done."[21] To accomplish this, for the presider, "the rule to be followed in selecting those who should have the floor is based on the idea that the purpose of the debate is to bring out all of the important points bearing on the issue at hand both pro and con."[22] The floor, therefore, will not necessarily be given in the order that delegates attempt to obtain it. The presider may even properly ask which position the one who has requested the floor is going to take before assigning the floor to him or her.

Discussion should cease only when it appears that to continue it will add no more to the understanding because it is becoming repetitious, or because all have spoken on the issue who wish to speak. Too-early use of procedural motions to cut off debate and reach an early vote should be avoided. Even if the best final action on a measure is to refer it, those to whom it is referred may be able to handle the referral more responsibly if the concerns and viewpoints of the body are heard. Even if the final action is to defeat the measure soundly, the body benefits from hearing the viewpoints of a responsible minority. A church which teaches the worth of all human souls has even more responsibility than a secular organization to hear the concerns of its minorities, even if it does not see fit to adopt the legislation they favor.

It is time to proceed to a vote when it is apparent that all useful discussion has been held. At this point it is appropriate for the presider to state that it appears further discussion is unnecessary and that without objection a vote will be taken. If many still wish to speak, but it appears that the discussion is becoming repetitious, it is then appropriate for a delegate to "move the previous question." This requires that the assembly vote on whether it is ready to take a final vote. If this motion carries, discussion immediately ends and the vote is taken. In other circumstances, other procedural motions may be appropriate, as described later. (The various methods of voting were discussed in chapter 5.)

Remembering that the purpose of parliamentary procedure is to assist the assembly to confer effectively and in an orderly fashion make decisions which reflect the will of the group, it is important for participants to become familiar with the motions which are used frequently. Only by understanding these can they be utilized appropriately in the deliberative process.

Frequently used motions include the following:

Motion to Adopt. "Main motions" are "the basic form of motion by which business is brought up and by which the assembly takes substantive action."[23] Most main motions are presented as resolutions, particularly if they are lengthy or complex.[24] They should be submitted in writing and be expressed affirmatively in concise unambiguous language.[25]

Object to Consideration. The purpose of this motion "is to enable the assembly to avoid a particular original main motion altogether when it believes it would be strongly undesirable for the motion even to come before the assembly."[26] It is applicable only to an original main motion or to hearing communications which are not from a superior body.

"Objection to consideration" must be made before any discussion of the motion has occurred or any other subsidiary motion has been made. It may be made without waiting to obtain the floor, does not require a second, and is not debatable. A two-thirds vote against consideration is required to sustain the objection.[27]

"Objection to consideration" has often been misused as a mechanism to defeat motions to which persons are strongly opposed. In these situations, however, the main motion should simply be voted down. The proper use of "objection to consideration" is only for contentious or slanderous subjects, or for repetitive and redundant or irrelevant motions that waste time.

To Amend. "The subsidiary motion to Amend is a motion to modify the wording—and within certain limits the meaning—of a pending motion before the pending motion itself is acted upon."[28] "It must in some way involve the same question that is raised by the motion to which it is applied."[29] A motion to amend proposes to add, delete, or to change words in the original motion.

There is actually no such entity as a "substitute" motion, but simply a motion to amend by substitution, in this case referring to a substitution of either the entire text or entire paragraphs of the main motion.

A secondary amendment may be made to a proposed first amendment to a main motion, but no further amendment may be made before action has been taken on the proposed amendments.

Discussion on the conference floor should always

be directed at the last proposal presented. When an amendment is proposed for a main motion, discussion is to be directed to the amendment; after a decision is made on the amendment, discussion resumes on the main motion. At times, Conferences become so involved in discussing amendments that the main motion does not receive proper attention. Therefore, too-early presentation of amendments should be avoided.

The last amendment proposed is voted on first, and the main motion itself is voted on last. If an amendment is passed (it requires a simple majority), it simply changes the statement of the main motion, which is then voted on as it has been amended. If the amendment fails, consideration of the main motion resumes as it was originally stated.

To Refer. "The subsidiary motion to *Commit or Refer* is generally used to send a pending question to a relatively small group of selected persons—a committee—so that the questions may be carefully investigated and put into better condition for the assembly to consider."[30] It should actually be used for this purpose, and not as a subterfuge for the actual defeat of a main motion. It is debatable only as to the desirability of the referral, the appropriateness of the body to which referral is proposed, and instructions that body is to follow.[31]

To Lay on the Table. The motion to lay on the table is proper only for laying a pending question aside temporarily so that something of more immediate urgency may be considered by the body.[32] It should be taken from the table at some future time when the interrupting business has been concluded.[33] "In ordinary assemblies, the motion to *Lay on the Table* is out of order if the evident intent is to kill or avoid dealing with a measure."[34]

If the assembly wishes to avoid a direct vote on a badly chosen main motion that cannot be either adopted or expressly rejected without undesirable consequences, the proper way to decline to take a position is through a motion to postpone indefinitely.[35] This motion effectively suppresses a measure throughout the entire current session of the assembly.

To Divide the Question. If a main motion consists of two or more parts that can be considered separately, the body may vote to consider them as two separate motions. If a single motion includes parts which are actually unrelated, the request of a single member of the assembly should be sufficient to have the different subjects considered separately.[36]

Move the Previous Question—This motion is used to bring the assembly to an immediate vote on one or more pending questions. It must be seconded, is not debatable, and requires a two-thirds vote of the body for passage.

Unless otherwise specified, the "previous question" applies to the last motion before the body, but it may be stated to include consecutively in reverse order any or all of a series of motions, including the main motion before the body. (For example, if a main motion [a], an amendment [b], a second amendment [c], and a motion for referral [d] are before the body, the motion for the previous question may include d, d&c, dc&b, or all four—it may *not* include d&b, c&a alone, etc.)[37]

The "previous question" is too often applied to "all matters before the body." When an amendment has been presented before adequate discussions has been held on the main motion, any motion to close debate should apply only to the amendment so discussion can be resumed on the main motion.

The proper use of the "previous question" is when debate has become repetitive, but not before adequate discussion has been held on a subject to hear all responsible points of view. It should *not* be used as a legislative maneuver to attempt to shut out presentation of other points of view. The motion is actually out of order, and should not be accepted by the presider, if both sides of a pro and con issue have not yet had opportunity to be heard.

Motion to Reconsider. A motion to reconsider allows a majority "to bring back for further consideration a motion which has already been voted on. The purpose of reconsidering a vote is to permit correction of hasty, ill-advised, or erroneous action, or to take into account added information or a changed situation that has developed since the taking of the vote."[38]

A motion to reconsider may be made only by a member who voted on the prevailing side the first time the vote was taken, but may be seconded by any member. It is debatable if the original motion was debatable, and the debate may include both the actual merits of the original question and any new information prompting the motion for reconsideration. If, however, the main motion was undebatable or if it had been voted upon as a result of voting the previous question, the motion to reconsider is undebatable.

A motion to reconsider is supposed to be made at a business session on the same or the following day on which the original motion was considered, except in the case of a standing quorum or committee which may make the motion at any later time in the same legislative assembly. When the motion is made within the proper time constraints, it need not be dealt with immediately, but the presider may note and assign it to a later time on the agenda. If the motion is made in a timely fashion, its actual consideration may come several days later in the same legislative assembly.

To Adjourn. A motion to adjourn means to close the meeting immediately, unless a specific time is mentioned. The motion may be made even while business is pending, except when a vote has been ordered or is being taken or the results announced. (If a question is pending at the time of adjournment, it should be taken up at the following session of the assembly.) However, while a motion to adjourn is pending, it is proper for the presider to make announcements, including description of the remaining business for the body, to receive motions to reconsider, to give notice or receive motions concerning the time of future sessions, and to engage in proper closing ceremonies. A meeting is not actually adjourned until the presider announces it is adjourned, and all members of the assembly should remain in their places and give full attention until that announcement is made.[39]

Point of Order. If a member feels that the rules of the assembly are being violated, a point of order may be raised, requesting the chair for a ruling and an enforcement of the proper rules. To be valid, the point must be made promptly at the time the rules breach occurs. The presider may then immediately rule that "The point is well taken," or "not well taken," or if in doubt may ask for parliamentary assistance or even a vote of the body on the point.

Points of order should be raised only on significant

breaches of the rights of the assembly. "It is undesirable to raise points of order on minor irregularities of a purely technical characer, if it is clear that no one's rights are being infringed upon and no real harm is being done to the proper transaction of business."[40]

Appeal the Decision of the Chair. By having been selected, the presider has been delegated the authority and duty to make necessary rulings on questions of parliamentary law. Any two members of the assembly, however, have the right to appeal the presider's ruling on a question, which then requires that the assembly make the final decision. If the matter upon which the presider has ruled is debatable, the merits of the ruling and the appeal are debatable; if the original matter is nondebatable, the vote on the appeal must be taken without debate.

If a member disagrees with a ruling of the chair affecting any substantial question, he should not hesitate to appeal. The situation is no more delicate than disagreeing with another member in debate. In the case of serious questions when proponents and opponents appear nearly equal, a presiding officer may welcome an appeal from his decision. By relieving the chair of responsibility in a strongly contested situation and placing it on the assembly itself, better relationships are often preserved.[41]

In cases of appeal, the motion should not be interpreted as indicating a lack of trust or support of the presider by the one making the motion, but simply that the member feels an error has been made. Members have no right to criticize a ruling of the chair unless they have appealed the decision.

Point of Personal Privilege. A question of privilege is proper at any time, if it is in regard to the wellbeing, safety, comfort, or reputation of the assembly or any member, and if it is sufficiently urgent to require immediate action. The member should indicate whether "I rise to a question of personal privilege," or "to a question of the privileges of the assembly," and then state the problem when recognized by the presider.[42] It is not proper to use this motion simply because of strong disagreement with statements of another speaker or to get the floor to attempt to speak instead of another member.

Point of Information or *Parliamentary Inquiry.* At any point a member may make a request of the presider to clarify the current parliamentary situation, to ask whether a certain motion would be in order, etc. This is a parliamentary inquiry. The member may also ask the presider to address a request for clarifying information to another member of the assembly to assist in understanding the issues under consideration. (All discussion in a deliberative assembly is directed toward the chair—members should not address each other directly. This allows the presider to keep control of the meeting, which is proper.) Particularly when the business before the body is non-debatable, as when the "previous question" has been ordered, "point of information" and "parliamentary inquiry" should be used strictly in the manner described. They are not proper ploys to engage in more discussion after a vote has been called for.

Motion to Suspend the Rules. A motion to suspend the rules is used to modify usual parliamentary procedure, usually to allow consideration of business that otherwise could not properly be considered at that time. Rules contained in the bylaws or standing *Rules of Order* cannot be suspended, no matter how large the vote in favor of doing so, because this act would be unfair to those church members not present in the assembly. Legislation by World Conference becomes policy for the entire church, and the rights of the church members not in the assembly must also be protected by following proper procedures in the Conference. Likewise, rules which protect the basic rights of the individual cannot be suspended, even by a unanimous vote.

Examples of rules which cannot be suspended would be votes on measures requiring certain advance notice for their consideration, or a rule that certain votes be taken by secret ballot, protecting a minority (even of one) from exposing how it voted. Rules which require a two-thirds vote for their passage or amendment require a two-thirds vote to be suspended—others may be suspended by majority vote.[43]

Time Limit on Debate. A motion to limit debate may take several forms. It may set a particular time for voting on the issue, or an overall time limit on the discussion. It may limit the number of speeches or the length of time devoted to individual speeches, either including or excluding the first pro and con speeches on an issue. It may apply only to the immediate question before the body or to all further matters to come before the assembly. Because limiting debate takes away the basic rights of all members to full discussion and may restrict a minority's right to present its case, it requires a two-thirds vote to be adopted.[44]

By having a good working knowledge of the principles of parliamentary procedure, including the meanings of the motions available for use, an alert member can utilize them to assist the assembly to deliberate responsibly and come to a decision which truly represents the will of the body. The misuse of too many procedural motions, points of order, etc., can result in the "tyranny of a minority"—obstructing the assembly from getting its necessary work done due to the time wasted. On the other extreme, however, is the "tyranny of the majority" which has the votes to repeatedly pass the "previous question" and other motions which prevent an equitable presentation of the viewpoints and concerns of the minority.

If the church, in legislative assemblies, is to express its concern for its mission, as well as recognize the importance of each person, it must proceed deliberately, with proper regard for the rights and concerns of all. Likewise, the success of the legislative body in deliberating effectively and coming to wise decisions depends on the knowledgeable participation of the individual delegates and their good will for one another.

SUMMARY

Large deliberative bodies require formalized "parliamentary procedures" to do business effectively and efficiently. These procedures should be adapted to the needs of the body with some flexibility given to the presider as long as the rights of both the majority and minorities are respected. Effective legislative sessions depend on delegates' familiarity with the procedures, particularly with the proper use of the various motions.

REFERENCES

1. Robert, Henry M., *Robert's Rules of Order,* 1981, xxvii.
2. Ibid.
3. Ibid.
4. Ibid., xxxix.
5. Ibid., xl.
6. Ibid., 9.
7. WCR 1091.
8. WCR 1156.
9. Robert's Rules, xlii.
10. Rules of Order III:18.
11. Ibid., V:33, VI:39, VII:47, VIII:53.
12. Ibid., VII:49, VIII:58.
13. Robert's Rules, 21.
14. Ibid., 29.
15. Ibid., 28.
16. Ibid., 29.
17. Ibid., 31.
18. Robert's Rules, 27.
19. Ibid., 328.
20. Ibid., 320.
21. Section by Fred Young, *A Guide for Good Priesthood Ministry,* Herald House (1971), 224.
22. Ibid.
23. Robert's Rules, 46.
24. Ibid., 87.
25. Ibid., 86.
26. Ibid., 227.
27. Ibid., 228.
28. Ibid., 108.
29. Ibid., 113.
30. Ibid., 140.
31. Ibid., 143.
32. Ibid., 177.
33. Ibid., 180.
34. Ibid., 178.
35. Ibid., 105.
36. Ibid., 232.
37. Ibid., 168.
38. Ibid., 265.
39. Ibid., 199.

40. Ibid., 215.
41. Ibid., 220-221.
42. Ibid., 191.
43. Ibid., 222.
44. Ibid., 163.

CHAPTER 13
The Revelatory Process

KEY CONCEPT: Revelation involves both divine disclosure and human understanding; the prophetic process is manifested when the church acts according to divine will and in revelatory statements through the prophet; statements are then considered according to established procedures for acceptance by the legislative body.

"The testimony of Jesus is the spirit of prophecy" (Rev. 19:10). This testimony grows as persons perceive the nature and purpose of God as revealed in Jesus the Christ, and then act accordingly. The church is founded on the concept of a consistent God who is revealed to humankind today as well as in the past,[1] and who enlists persons to respond actively in the prophetic process.

The prophetic process is much more than merely predicting the course of events. It means that we should look at the world through the eyes of faith, and under the impress of the Spirit of God, discern to the greatest degree possible the issues being raised and the nature of the choices put before us.[2]

Acting and speaking prophetically, manifesting the mind and will of God, require that God's will be known. This is possible insofar as the divine will is disclosed, and to the extent to which people comprehend that disclosure.

Divine revelation...involves both divine disclosure and human understanding....There is no true revelation until his self-disclosure is matched by sufficient insight on the part of those who see him at work for them to know something about who he is and what is going on.[3]

Persons are prophetic who can discern the nature and purposes of God and then speak and act in accord with them. The church is called to be a prophetic body of people—expressing the nature and purposes of God in its actions and relationships in the world of its time.

When the church asks itself and wrestles with *who* it is as a people of God, *what* it is as the body of Christ, and what it is to *do* to engage in God's mission, it is being prophetic. When it receives answers to these questions from a revelatory document, a sermon, a report, a discussion of issues on the conference floor, or other sources, it is receiving prophetic ministry.

To act prophetically requires the church to be engaged in specific prophetic ministries. The World Conference engages in the prophetic process as it makes decisions regarding programs and policies that use resources and time in the manner designed of God.

Any person may express prophetic ministry in his or her own area of functioning. "God has no grandchildren"—only children. Each of God's children can have a direct relationship with God which may involve divine disclosure and individual understanding and response.

President W. Wallace Smith stated in a World Conference sermon:

The word of God can come in various ways:

1. Through direct revealment in (a) open vision, (b) audible voice, or (c) the still [silent] voice of inspiration.
2. Through subtle revealment in (a) the testimony of others, (b) observance of natural phenomena, and (c) intuition.
3. Through the exercise of (a) wisdom, (b) logic, and (c) good reasoning.[4]

The same understanding can come to different individuals in different ways; for example, to one by the still voice of inspiration, to another by receiving that person's testimony, or to another by serious study and reasoning. Persons need to be open and sensitive to the disclosure of God from any source if they are to act prophetically.

The church affirms the right, and indeed the responsibility, for all individuals to come personally to an understanding of God's will for them—both as individuals and as a part of the whole body of Christ. The church is strengthened as all members seek to be open and to respond to the revelation of God in their lives.

The church corporately, however, takes an identity which is greater than the sum of the individuals in it. The belief that God is continuing to be revealed to individuals is shared among most denominations. The Reorganized Church of Jesus Christ of Latter Day Saints also affirms that in its corporate existence the revelation of God is received for the benefit of the church and humankind. Revelation given to the corporate church has significance for the church as a whole, each jurisdictional segment, and for each individual member. This significance should be considered at each level.

While any person can merit the gift of prophecy, only those appointed and ordained to the offices of presidency are to be revelators to the people at large. This principle has applied since the earliest days of the church. It means that in the jurisdictions of the church, the administrators with presidential authority are the ones authorized to present statements identified as revelatory guidance for their jurisdictions. For messages to be considered as instruction to the entire church and for inclusion in the Doctrine and Covenants, the president and prophet of the church is the sole revelator.

Written collections of prophetic statements are authorized only at the World Church level. No collection other than the Doctrine and Covenants is authorized. Any other collection is specifically discouraged in WCR 709.

Many think of the role of the prophet only in terms of documents which are presented as revelations to World Conferences from time to time, but the prophetic function is also seen in the continuing leadership given to the church. It is manifested most thoroughly in the day-to-day administration of the church's affairs in accord with the purposes of God. It should be seen in the reports given to the World Conference of the activities of the Presidency (and of other leaders). It should also be seen in the overall program of ministries presented for adoption by Conferences, in sermons, and in other counsel given to the church. This is not to imply that all the actions and statements of any person, including any church leader, will perfectly express the mind and will of God. Rather, God's will should be expressed throughout all aspects of the church's life, its members and its leaders, not just in occasional statements identified as revelation.

None of the foregoing detracts from the importance of specific revelatory statements given to the church at specific times. These are of extreme importance in the life of the church. If specific statements are to be formally recognized and accepted as revelation by the church, they must be approved as such by a World Conference.

The prophet may present a statement of the mind and will of God to the body at the time and in the manner he feels best. Through the years, the tradition has developed for prophets to present revelatory statements first to the quorums, orders, and councils for their consideration privately before presentation to the body as a whole. After these bodies approve them (according to procedures established within the bodies), they are then presented to the entire World Conference in a legislative session. In more recent years, the documents have been shared simultaneously with the mass meetings of the elders and of the Aaronic priesthood and with the delegate sessions—in other words, to the entire World Conference in its prelegislative units. This has shown the prophet's great respect for the maturity of all portions of the body.

While the prophet determines how a revelatory statement is presented for consideration, the legislative body may decide how it will consider the document, for example, as a whole, by paragraph, line by line, or other. The ultimate action of the World Conference, however, is to accept or reject the document as a whole. It cannot be amended except by the prophet.

The World Conference may take three legislative actions with regard to a revelatory statement:

• Accept a statement as the mind and will of God (or not accept it).

• Approve the statement for inclusion in the Doctrine and Covenants.

• Provide for carrying out any actions called for in the statement, such as ordinations, changes in quorums, etc.

These actions traditionally are included in the same motion, but occasionally have been divided into separate motions.

Members should vote their acceptance of a revelatory statement only after careful and prayerful consideration of its content. Agreeing that something is the mind and will of God places serious obligations on the church and on individuals, and such agreement should not be given lightly. A confirming vote given after thorough consideration is a meaningful testimony to its truth, but a vote to approve given automatically is an empty form.

It should not be surprising if every revelatory document meets with some initial division of feeling about its validity. It has been said that "revelation does not occur in a vacuum." It comes in response to issues with which the people are wrestling, over questions on which they are divided. If there were already complete unanimity and understanding by the members—if it were something everyone already knew—the "revelation" would be unnecessary and meaningless. When answers come which are different from people's convictions it is not surprising that even those of goodwill might not immediately be able to recognize those answers as being from God. People should live according to their convictions developed out of their careful and prayerful understandings of God's will. Those convictions should not be abandoned or changed lightly—even when a statement is presented as revelation. But conviction needs to be balanced with sufficient receptivity to new light to accept that which is of God.

Careful consideration of a revelatory document, with thorough study and discussion, does not imply distrust of the prophet, but can add interpretive insights and understanding by the body and give a confirming witness. Active knowledgeable *consent,* not just *assent,* is essential if a statement is to guide actions which can be seen as prophetic. A vote of approval should indicate a serious intent to live out the principles stated, for it is in the living out that the real confirmation comes.

The procedures which have been described embody the principle that revelation involves both divine disclosure and human understanding. The prophet's statement is presented as a divine disclosure. Human understanding is expressed in the legislative processes of formal acceptance and subsequently in actions, both individual and corporate, which are in accord with the will of God as it has been presented.

In the matter of accepting revelation, the Saints apparently have succeeded in combining the will of God and the will of the people. This . . . forms the very basis, the source of nourishment, and the means of development and progress within the Reorganized Church of Jesus Christ of Latter Day Saints. God forbid that we shall ever lose either the will or the ability to allow his Spirit to guide our destiny as individuals and as a corporate body.[5]

SUMMARY

The revelatory process involves both divine disclosure and human understanding. God's disclosure comes at points of human need for guidance, usually on questions persons are dealing with, and divided over. Those who preside are authorized to express revelatory counsel for their jurisdictions. Only that expressed by the prophet for the entire church is authorized for publication in the Doctrine and Covenants, after having been considered by the World Conference. The prophetic process is expressed both in specific revelatory statements and in ways of living which reveal the mind and will of God.

REFERENCES

1. Aleah G. Koury, *The Truth and the Evidence*, Herald House (1965), 9.
2. W. Wallace Smith, 1974 World Conference Sermon, *Saints Herald* (May 1974), 294.
3. F. Henry Edwards, *Fundamentals*, Herald House (1948), Second Edition, 39.
4. Smith sermon, 294.
5. Smith sermon, 293.

CHAPTER 14

International Implications of World Conferences

KEY CONCEPTS: The World Conference needs to develop procedures which are as inclusive as possible and in accordance with universal principles.

"God is no respecter of persons; but in every nation he that feareth him, and worketh righteousness, is accepted with him" (Acts 10:34-35). In recent years, the church has been struggling with the meaning of this scripture. The struggle has demanded that the church define which elements of its functioning and forms of worship are basic and essential to the gospel, and which may be adapted to varying cultures and situations.

There are elements of the gospel—such as the need for persons to acknowledge God's dominion—that are universal and should be expressed by the church in *all* cultures where it exists. "If the gospel is true at all, it is true all the time and in every part of the world."[1] However, the church needs to understand the unchangeable *essentials* of the gospel and the *forms* of its expression which can vary. The specific means of expressing the essential elements will vary in different cultural settings. The same basic and universal truth may be expressed in many different forms. There is no limit to the number of ways for expressing the basic call to love one another as neighbors. There is no limit to the number of ways for people to acknowledge God's dominion as they worship and as they relate to one another, to earth's resources, and to God.

"The gospel is never a prisoner of a single culture or national tradition. It lies above each of these, and the church must immerse itself in the milieu of every nation to carry out its mission."[2] This means understanding and respecting the distinctiveness and richness within the many cultures of the world. "Becoming a world church requires us to plant the seed of the gospel in other lands and take the risk of letting the people there interpret the gospel as it has meaning for them and package it in forms of expression which are indigenous."[3]

Taking the gospel to other cultures enriches the church as well as the persons in those cultures. Deeper understandings can come for everyone as the church sees new ways that its long-held beliefs are expressed in the lives of persons in other parts of the world. On the other hand, the inadequacy of other long-revered concepts can become apparent if they prove to be inappropriate for the life situations of people elsewhere. The church has had to learn not to try to impose "Western" cultural traditions on those parts of the world where it has been working to plant the gospel. "The problems arising from our work among the diverse cultures of our missions have made some wish that we had never ventured so far abroad. In the long run, however, if we are to be the Church of Jesus Christ we have no other choice."[4]

A statement by the First Presidency at the 1980 World Conference should guide the thoughts of the church in this regard:

We of the First Presidency are anxious to reaffirm our commitment to the objective of truly becoming a World Church. Our program of missionary emphasis for the decade of the eighties anticipates significant expansion in the areas of the world which until now we have only begun to realize. One of the consequences of such expansion, of course, will be the increasingly international character of our World Conferences. We are concerned that this international emphasis be properly addressed and that issues of a parochical or even national interest not unduly occupy the time and energy of the World Conference.[5]

Part of the process of planting the seed of the gospel in other cultures involves a certain amount of "letting go" of centralized decision-making.

It is important that the various local jurisdictions of the body be free to make decisions and engage in the program necessary to build the kingdom. The decision-making responsibility and accountability should be kept as close as possible to the legislative and administrative level where it is to be implemented.... Whatever provincialism we have had—and it has been considerable—must be revised in the ever increasing understanding of our call to be a world church.[6]

Some ask then, "What holds the church together?" The answer is the overriding commitment to Jesus Christ, and specifically such factors as (1) the willingness to respect and receive ministry from World Church officers and other assigned representatives; (2) common acceptance of and willingness to live by the Bible, Book of Mormon, and Doctrine and Covenants; and (3) participation in and willingness to abide by the actions of the World Conference.[7]

Just as important as the need for persons everywhere to observe certain basic principles of the gospel to be identified as part of the body of Christ is the need for the church's Conferences to express a world view. The church must come to grips with the question, What is essential to the faith? and understand that the testimony of Jesus Christ can be lived out in the life settings of all peoples. This principle is easy to state, but even easier to forget as the World Conference does its business. Problems in acting as a "world" Conference are seen in many areas, such as systems of representation, language barriers, the procedures used, and in the provincial nature of the issues considered.

Representation. Many persons from other nations find it difficult to travel to Conferences in the United States because of distance, time, cost, and travel regulations. The representation of these jurisdictions is then diminished in number. Their delegations are often completed by selecting persons from central areas who are to represent them, but these persons usually have little or no knowledge of the areas they are representing. If a delegation cannot be filled by those who actually live in the jurisdiction, persons should be selected who can express as accurately as possible the concerns and views of the residents of those jurisdictions.

Even when they are able to travel to a World Conference, members from distant cultures may be overwhelmed, experiencing sufficient "cultural shock" to diminish their ability to participate fully as delegates. If the Conference is to be truly a World Conference, it must give attention to these problems.

Language. English has been the language of all World Conferences, not by official action, but because it has apparently been assumed to be the language which should be used. English is not universally understood, however, even by many intelligent and world-minded people of other cultures. Only a portion of the Conference materials is translated into any language other than English. This makes some reports, written legislation, minutes, and other printed matter difficult to understand by non-English-speaking participants. In the translations which are broadcast during Conference sessions, the unavoidable time lag makes it difficult for them to participate in the usual conferring and legislative processes.

Procedures. The processes of decision-making in the church are currently derived from a Western orientation, and many who come to Conference are used to making decisions differently. Some have different understandings of what is polite and respectful behavior between persons and find the usual methods of legislative participation actually repugnant. These methods may seem to be disrespectful to the presider and to the other members of the body.

Even if the legislative procedures are accepted, quick response is often required to enter the process to make a motion or to speak on an issue. If one is waiting for a translation, this is impossible. Many issues have been discussed and votes ordered without the non-English-speaking delegates having been able to participate in the discussion, even when they have so desired. The Conference has given limited recognition to this problem in recent years by extending to some of these delegates the courtesy of the opportunity to speak even after votes have been taken. The random selection procedure of the computerized system of registering for participation has significantly alleviated the situation. The church must develop procedures which permit the full involvement of all members in the conferring processes *before decisions are made,* in spite of differences in language and culture.

Provincial subject matter and decisions. Many matters brought to World Conference are not of general concern to the World Church, though they may be proper concerns to certain areas of the church, such as the United States and Canada. This problem often arises because these jurisdictions have no legislative forum between the level of regions or stakes and the World Conference before which these issues may be brought. They are therefore brought to the World Conference. As a result, some of the issues dealt with at World Conferences are primarily the business of the church in the United States and/or Canada, and are neither comprehended by, nor significant to, the delegates from other parts of the world.

For example, in 1972, a resolution was brought to the World Conference to approve an official Liahona theme song and insignia for use on college campuses.[8] These had little meaning for persons outside of the United States and Canada, and the resolution was referred to the campus ministry office.

Much discussion was held in the 1970s about air conditioning the Auditorium. A proposal for installing air conditioning was presented at the 1976 Conference but turned down by the delegates because it would have significantly benefited only the center place. With the immense physical needs of people in many parts of the world, and the church's ministries limited by available funds, air conditioning the Auditorium was not thought to deserve a high priority.

In some instances, problems develop because actions which seem logical and proper in Western culture may be interpreted differently in other cultures. The meaning of acts and patterns of living are determined by the meaning vested in them. An action which may be interpreted in one culture as an act of friendship or brotherly concern may in another be considered immoral and associated with a way of life that is opposed to the values for which Christians must stand. For this reason we must be careful in our legislative attempts to define conduct.[10]

Most decisions at World Conferences are made out of the understandings of Western cultures. The body often does not comprehend the implications of those decisions for other cultures. In these circumstances the problem goes beyond that of a minority simply not having its position adopted, for a decision made with the understanding of Western cultures may seem sinful in the understanding of other cultures.

At the 1968 Conference, a resolution was presented that would have expressed church approval of social dancing. It did not take into account that in some cultures dancing is a routine prelude to more intimate activity, with implications not intended by those from the culture where the resolution was written. After consideration, the Conference accepted a resolution from the high priests quorum that included the following statements:

WHEREAS, There are wide variations between nations and cultures in the meaning and moral influence of certain patterns of conduct, and

WHEREAS, The international and intercultural nature of the church and the World Conference therefore make it inadvisable for the Conference to legislate specific patterns of personal conduct,...therefore be it

RESOLVED, That this Conference affirms its nature as a legislative body representing a worldwide membership, and declares its intention to exercise care in the introduction and consideration of legislative matters, that they be of universal value and application; and that it further desires to reflect this affirmation in the terminology and phraseology of its enactments....[11]

Over the years the church has considered a number of resolutions concerning peace, war, and the use of force, and has updated its position statements with changing circumstances. However, such resolutions with international implications must be worded very carefully to avoid potential problems for members in some parts of the world. For example, the 1968 Conference declined to adopt a resolution urging members to seek noncombatant service during military conflicts.[12] This position is legal under United States laws, but would be considered criminal for members subject to the laws of some other nations.

Resolving these problems will involve changes in several areas—particularly provision for dealing with legislative matters at other levels and for adequate conferring so that the body will understand what its decisions mean in the various parts of the world. The church needs to determine which principles are universal and basic to its faith, then develop methods of conferring which will enable participation of the broad worldwide base of the church in the decision-making process.

Problems are often correctly interpreted as *opportunities*, provided they receive a creative response. Those discussed in the foregoing have given the church opportunity to respond in ways which have been very useful and gratifying. The First Presidency has stated that

the World Church leaders have been aware of the need for increasing dialogue with the international churches for some time and have been meeting this need in various ways. We have held...Asia-Pacific Conferences in which the national church leaders in the Orient, South Pacific, and India Fields have met with members of the First Presidency, Council of Twelve, and Presiding Bishopric to confer on the unique contributions and challenges which these non-Western cultures bring to the Restoration.[13]

Similar meetings have been held with European, African, and Latin American church leaders, and it is anticipated that these types of meetings will continue on a regular basis "to facilitate further intercultural understanding and World Church dialogue."[14]

In national and mission conferences, participants have learned that the Restoration, having brought gospel truths to other cultures, has been greatly enriched by their understandings and their cultural expressions. This has become evident also in some of the non-legislative forums which have been held in connection with some of the World Conferences in recent years—such as the International Women's Forums, International Leaders' Assemblies, and various leaders' seminars. In these forums, there has been effective conferring about how universal human concerns are handled in the various cultures, and how the gospel addresses those concerns in those cultures. The church has been succeeding in its efforts to bcome a truly World Church in some thrilling ways. This can simply be a foretaste of further successes to come.

Much of the responsibility for carrying the message of Christ throughout the world and bringing to the assembled body the understandings of cultures rests with the Council of Twelve Apostles.[15] Their inspiring Statement of Commitment at the 1980 World Conference is commended for study in its entirety, including such affirmations as the following:

183

We live in a most remarkable era—an age filled with unusual opportunities and challenges. The vision we seek to magnify is joining with the Holy Spirit in the dynamic fashioning of Christ-like relationships among all peoples.

In recent years the Restoration Church has sought to respond faithfully to the call to be a world church. In this interdependent world we are affirming that God did make of one blood all nations and that "there is neither Jew nor Greek, there is neither bond nor free, there is neither male nor female; for ye are all one in Christ Jesus" (Gal. 3:28). It is our conviction that in Christ there are no racial, social, economic, educational, or other barriers to the one great fellowship of all humankind...

We have discovered that the gospel of Jesus Christ is best presented in cultural expressions and forms familiar to those who receive it. If the universal truths of the gospel are to be grasped, individuals must be able to hear and to respond to the gospel in ways they can comprehend...As they are won to Christ and grow in understanding they are able to join more fully in the communion of the World Church.

If faithful to its mission, each local segment of the church will be rooted in Jesus Christ even while standing within the culture in which it exists. Cultures differ from one another, yet God has no favorites among them. "For, behold, the Lord grants to all nations, those of their own nation and tongue, to teach his word, in wisdom, all that he sees fit that they should have" (Alma 15:59).

Persons of whatsoever nation, tribe, or people should have opportunity to express their selfhood within the body of Christ. It is difficult to disunite our national and tribal traditions from our worship, structure, and polity. This is the case in every society. Their validity is determined by their faithfulness to the essence of the Gospel of Jesus Christ. Peter needed a vision from God before he could say, "God hath showed me that I should not call any man common or unclean....Of a truth I perceive that God is no respecter of persons" (Acts 10:28, 34). We bear witness that as we respect the Holy Spirit's ministry, diverse peoples mature as disciples in dignity and integrity. They grow in ability to exercise wise decision-making in harmony with the divine gifts of their culture...

Each cultural expression of the church is a part of the World Church: for there is one Lord and one body of Christ. Each individual and every gathering of the Saints lives out the common faith in the midst of pluralism and cultural diversity. For the God-given gifts of every person and every culture we give thanks. The people of Christ from all nations blend into a worldwide body enriched by the ministry of the Holy Spirit. . . .

We call upon the whole church

To discover the joy of witnessing for Jesus Christ through living out the will of God for our day and time.

To commit willingly full allegiance and all talents and resources to God's work.

To proclaim enthusiastically that Jesus is the Christ of all peoples, that all societies may be redeemed and purified by divine love.

To receive joyfully the gifts of every culture where God's people may be found.

To join with God in loosing the shackles of social status, privilege, and divisions.

To listen intently, to respond genuinely to the cries of the vulnerable, such as the poor, the oppressed, the powerless, and the lonely.

As a growing, expanding, world-wide body committed to Jesus Christ, let us sound clear notes of joy, hope, peace, and love to an anguished world; let us evidence the enthusiasm that has always been characteristic of God's people; let us undergird each moment with expectation of the great things yet to be achieved with God.

SUMMARY

The procedures of World Conferences have been developed out of a Western orientation, and the subjects considered have often been of parochial interest to the church in the United States and Canada. Members from non-Western cultures often are unable to attend Conferences, and the participation of those attending is limited by barriers of language and unfamiliar procedures. Delegates need to take into account the implications of the legislation in various cultures. All members need to develop a "world view," an appreciation that the gospel can be expressed in many languages, and lived out in the varied cultures and customs of people throughout the world.

REFERENCES

1. Clifford Cole, "Theological Perspectives of World Mission," *Saints' Herald* (July 1971), 13.
2. Duane Couey, "From the First Presidency," *Saints Herald* (July 1975), 4.
3. Clifford Cole, "Explorations in Becoming a World Church," *Saints Herald* (August 1978), 20.
4. Clifford Cole, "Theological Perspectives of World Mission," *Saints' Herald* (July 1971), 13.
5. 1980 WCB, 304.
6. *Perspectives,* 13.
7. Ibid., 60.
8. 1972 WCB, 251.
9. 1976 WCB, 225, 234.
10. *Perspectives,* 60.
11. 1968 WCB, 147, 270, 285.
12. Ibid., 268.
13. 1980 WCB, 304.
14. Ibid.
15. *Saints Herald* (May 1980), 8.

CHAPTER 15

Problems of Present Procedures Alternatives, and Possible Future Directions

KEY CONCEPT: Within the limits of church law and of applicable laws of nations, World Conference procedures must be continuously evaluated and updated in response to changing times and circumstances.

World Conference is the highest legislative body in the church and, as such, must be organized with reference to this function. The body should be small enough to function as a true deliberative assembly, yet large enough to allow for the expression of wide-ranging points of view. The Conference structure and how it relates to this function must be continuously examined in light of the concept of the church as a theocratic democracy and historic emphasis on the role of common consent in the decision-making process.[1]

The goal of developing the best structure for World Conferences is a "moving target." What works best at one point in time may not be appropriate even a few years later. This is true because the people change who come to World Conferences. More people come from more varied cultures, speak a greater number of languages, have different levels of sophistication in methods of decision-making, and carry different concerns from those who participated in earlier Conferences. There will always be a need to adapt the forms of World Conferences to the abilities and needs of the changing membership if the body is to be faithful in expressing the unchanging truths of the gospel in varieties of situations.

To examine the church's current structures and procedures and find problems is not to criticize their development and use in the past. It is simply to recognize that times change. Forms and procedures which were entirely appropriate in the past may not be adequate in present or future situations. In the earliest days of the church, conferences could be simple meetings of the entire membership. With a worldwide membership now numbering many thousands, it is obvious that the structures and procedures used then could not be utilized today.

The size of World Conferences has been of continuing concern. When Conferences are too large, some problems may develop:

The facilities may be inadequate to provide all delegates a seat from which they can participate effectively, particularly in general sessions. Almost any system of gaining recognition presents difficulties because of competition for access to the floor. Those who are not conveniently seated in the chamber, those who are not experienced, those who are not forward, and particularly those who do not understand English well, have limited opportunities for participation.

In addition, the large size of an assembly prevents thorough conferring or exchanging of views because of the difficulty of getting participants together. Time is insufficient for more than a fraction of the delegates to be heard on any given issue. Also, many have cultural inhibitions (especially women from certain cultures) and others have "stage fright" at the thought of speaking at a large public meeting.

The varied backgrounds and preparation of the participants create significant problems in the operation of World Conferences. Many good members come to Conference without knowing how to participate effectively, how to follow parliamentary procedure, or how to use motions and methods of discussion. This is true, not only of members from throughout the world, but of those from Western cultures. Conference procedures are just as "foreign" to some of the Western subcultures (such as some racial and ethnic minorities) as to those from thousands of miles away.

Another problem which sometimes arises out of the background of the participants is what could be termed "too much" preparation. This may take at least two forms:

Certain issues, primarily of a parochial nature, may have been present for some time, even spanning several World Conferences, and have had extensive discussion by many of the members. Words, phrases, and references may have special meaning for those who have discussed the issues many times before, but are meaningless and illogical to others who have not previously discussed them.

Other issues may be of world interest, but have already been discussed extensively by many delegates due to their proximity to the location of the Conference or other places where they can gather in sufficient strength for such discussions. These persons often develop firm positions and legislative strategies which prevent real and open conferring by the time Conference convenes.

While *conferring* on matters of concern should rarely be discouraged for a group, taking firm positions on issues in which others have an interest should be avoided until those others have been properly heard in the World Conference. Those with the advantage of conferring outside of Conference need to avoid actions which may tend to exclude participation by those without this advantage. Part of the respect owed to the value and rights of all other members is to remain open to hearing their concerns and views before making final decisions on matters of mutual interest.

Parliamentary procedure itself tends to develop "win-lose" types of situations, with debating instead of conferring, and majority votes instead of consensus actions. Specific problems that often arise include the following:

A. Limitation of options occurs in the wording of legislation. Parliamentary procedure functions best to help a body choose among only a very few ways of stating a legislative action. Amendment of resolutions is possible, but becomes unwieldy and time consuming if numerous options are presented. Rarely is there opportunity for the kind of conferring that can refine the statements to the best wording to state the intent of the assembly.

When voting, limited numbers of options can even lead to "accidental majorities." An example is when one segment of the assembly may vote against a proposal because it does not go far enough to satisfy them, and another because it goes too far, combining for a majority against the measure. A *real* majority may have wanted at least what was provided for in the resolution.

B. Polarization tends to develop on issues with debating as opposed to conferring. There is a lining up of power blocks rather than working issues through for the benefit of all.

C. Tyranny of the majority occurs when it acts to pass resolutions by using procedural motions which lead to rapid decisions, preventing the voices of minorities from being heard. The real test of democracy is not so much that the majority rules, but that the minorities' rights are also protected. Also, as stated elsewhere, the support of the minority for decisions cannot be expected if their viewpoints and concerns have not been honestly considered in the decision.

D. Tyranny of the minority, who can use argumentative amendments and procedural motions to occupy the time of the assembly even after issues have been adequately discussed, and prevent the majority from moving to fuller consideration of other issues.

E. Tyranny of the presider can occur, particularly in small congregations by a presider who does not follow parliamentary procedure or respect the rights of the members. This includes monopolizing the time, stating questions in a biased fashion, misinforming as to church law and policies, exercising power coercively, and other. The presider may not intend to abuse the rights of the body, but may simply not know how to lead a meeting properly, or may be so certain of knowing what is best for the group that an attempt is made to control decisions by the manner of presiding.

Time limitations are a real problem in all conferences. Some problems include the following:

A. The required business items (such as receiving reports, passing a budget, and sustaining officers), in addition to submitted legislation, often result in an agenda too crowded for sufficient evaluation of each item.

B. The budget is usually considered at a World Conference fairly early, before some program items can be considered which might require modification of the budget. The body, then, tends to react negatively to these items rather than reconsider the budget which has already been passed.

On the other hand, the budget cannot be left until too late in the agenda for its proper consideration. And even if items requiring funding were passed before consideration of the budget, they could not be included in the budget presentation in the same manner as other budget items.

C. When time is running short, late in the Conference, motions of referral are frequently utilized before substantive discussion of items has occurred. Even if referral is the best action, the assembly benefits from an exchange of views. The committee to which the item is referred can often do its job better if the discussion of the body can be used as a starting point for its work.

Elections (for example, for boards and committees) from among multiple candidates for more than one position offer real problems for determining the will of the body:

A. If persons are nominated for one position only, then the best qualified or preferred candidates may all have been nominated for the same position, none of them, then, are available for the other positions.

B. "Runoffs" between top vote-getters for a position may reflect a situation in which they represent a minority preference. This can occur if the majority has spread its votes among a larger number of nominees who have the philosophies or characteristics preferred by the majority.

C. Voting on all of the candidates for one of the positions, on all of the remaining candidates for the next position, etc., can occupy an inordinate amount of time, and still present the same problems with "runoffs."

Other problems exist, of course, not covered in the foregoing discussion, and new problems will emerge as the church forges ahead into new areas of endeavor. This will call for new responses on the part of the body. The ways that problems are handled will witness to the faithfulness of the body to the message of Christ.

The solutions to problems of conferring within a church which is growing in numbers and cultural diversity are not simple, and few perfect solutions ever exist. All potential solutions involve weighing advantages against disadvantages, considering the needs of the many while protecting the rights of the few. Constructive, creative approaches will be required to do the business of the church in the best manner possible.

Past and recent changes (and undoubtedly future changes) include consideration of the following:

A. Reducing the total size of World Conferences, providing for more co-equal conferring and working together by delegates from the many cultures represented. The need to control the size of World Conferences is recognized by almost everyone. The best method of doing it is not clear, however.

B. Dividing World Conferences into working legislative committees to confer on certain subjects and bring them to plenary sessions after they have been refined.

C. Lengthening the total time devoted to World Conferences to allow more conferring in depth and more deliberate decision-making. This may be done by extending the time of the Conference itself, or by expanding the associated conferring activities such as the hearing committees, the quorum and delegate sessions, the leaders' assemblies, or other, prior to the actual Conference.

D. Diminishing the frequency of World Conferences, with greater advance preparation by delegates and subordinate jurisdictions.

E. Restricting the subjects considered in World Conferences to matters of general concern to the church as a whole. This would require dealing with matters of interest to subordinate jurisdictions in conferences of those jurisdictions.

F. Establishing additional conferences at national, regional, or tribal levels, or involving other logical groupings of members in legislative meetings.

G. Developing new procedures which promote the processes of conferring instead of debating, leading to more refinement of legislation and consensus-building than is practicable with existing systems of parliamentary procedure.

H. Changing the methods of elections for boards and committees, and of elected officers in subordinate jurisdictions. Possibilities include "preferential balloting" systems in which ballots are marked for candidates in order of the voters' preferences—if the voter's first choice is eliminated from consideration, the ballot is counted for the voter's second choice, etc. (This system functions well in Australia.)

I. Retaining flexibility in organization and procedures of Conferences, within the limits of church law.

The World Conference has the power to structure itself to do business most effectively within the limits of church law and of applicable laws of nations. Over the years, several groups have explored refinements and alternatives for conferring. The Conference Organization and Procedures Committee, a standing committee of the World Conference, recommends procedures for selecting and certifying delegates' credentials, as well as for conducting Conference business. General church officers give continuing attention to the needs of the church in its decision-making processes. Their sound advice and recommendations for conferring have guided the church on many occasions.

Future Conferences may forthrightly shape a parliamentary-conferring system that nurtures common consent, leaving a historical record both exciting and sobering to contemplate. If that happens it will be because the Conference will have freed itself to discern, explore, and act on such issues as ought to occupy the time and attention of a prophetic world-wide church.[2]

The participants in World Conferences, and other conferences, should see the ultimate role of the Conference as an instrument of the church's mission. This is well stated in a quotation from the 1974 Conference Organization and Procedures Committee report:

The church is called to live in the world witnessing to the redeeming love of God and is called to perpetuate in its own life the ministries it discerns in the life of its Lord, Jesus Christ. Every structural form the church takes must facilitate this basic function. Thus, at root, the World Conference is to be understood as an instrument of the church's mission. Its primary role is to facilitate the achievement of that mission. Ultimately, the validity of what it does will be determined by the extent to which the mission of the church has been served.[3]

SUMMARY

Structures and procedures which are appropriate for one time in the church's life may not be appropriate for another, as a result of changing circumstances in the life of the church and the world. All systems are compromises between ideals—size small enough to allow all to participate, but large enough to encompass all viewpoints—time which is adequate to explore ideas thoroughly, yet handling a maximum of business in a limited period—full protection of the rights of the majority as well as those of the minority, and other. Conferences need to be seen by members as an instrument to accomplish the church's mission.

REFERENCES

1. Anita Butler, "The Functions of World Conference," *Saints Herald* (January 1976), 30.
2. Richard P. Howard, "Reflections on World Conference," *Saints Herald* (May 1976), 41.
3. 1974 WCB, 175.

CHAPTER 16

Debriefing of World Conference

KEY CONCEPT: Following a World Conference, its events and decisions should be reviewed carefully and systematically in the jurisdictions in order for the significance of those decisions of the work in each area to be understood.

The basic message of the church is the faith affirmation that there is a loving God, whose nature and purpose are revealed in Jesus Christ, who demonstrated his love for humankind by becoming one with them. The church shares the good news that "God is in Christ reconciling the world unto himself" (II Cor. 5:19), testifying that life can be new in Christ, with purpose and hope for every person.

"The validity of the testimony of Jesus Christ which the church offers to the world springs from the integrity and coherence in the total life-style of the fellowship which calls itself the body of Christ"[1]—the consistency with which it shows in various cultures what it means to "bear one another's burdens," "love your enemies," be the "salt of the earth," and to be the "city set upon a hill." As these gospel principles are manifested differently, but faithfully, in a variety of cultural settings their universality is demonstrated. This validates the church's mission "to interpret and represent the Christian witness as the ideal life-style for everyone everywhere."[2]

For the church to manifest universal principles in a variety of settings, it must have a strong organic unity. "The spirit of unity must prevail if my church is to survive these perilous times and continue as a viable force in the world, fulfilling its destiny" (D. and C. 150:12). The church is a body with many members (I Corinthians, chapter 12), but the members are to act as one body. The whole human body has right and left hands with different capabilities; their functioning must be coordinated by the head and eyes to work effectively. The head must likewise coordinate the movement of the feet if the body is to maintain its balance and move in the desired direction.

The considerable pluralism in the church is a great problem if members follow their own programs without regard to the whole. It is an immense strength when people with diverse talents and understandings coordinate their efforts in the work, each one serving as he or she is most capable. This can happen only with a unified program under unified leadership which recognizes the value and contribution of each part.

Unified leadership for the parts of the corporate body is essential for witnessing of Jesus Christ with integrity and coherence. The identity of the church as one body depends on the willingness of its parts to accept the authority of the World Conference, and of the World Church officers and their assigned representatives.

"The World Conference is constituted according

to the provisions of the rules of representation and is empowered to act for the entire church."[3] World Conferences would be an immense exercise in futility if there were no provision for carrying out their decisions throughout the church.

The First Presidency is authorized and responsible for this task.

The Presidency is the leading quorum in the church...the duty of presiding over the church devolves on that quorum...it is the prerogative of the President to preside over the whole church, to bear the responsibility of the care and oversight of the work of the church in all its different departments; and through the constituted officers of the church in their various callings, according to the laws, rules, and regulations in force and recognized by the church.[4]

World Conferences make decisions which set overall policies and program priorities, but cannot legislate the details of programs. Implementation of programs under the direction of the First Presidency is largely delegated and decentralized. This means that departments and jurisdictions have the prerogative of developing their program specifics within the parameters established by World Conferences, and as interpreted by the First Presidency.

Conferences need to carry out the processes of conferring and decision-making responsibly, with consideration of the views and concerns across the breadth of the church, both geographically and philosophically, before decisions are made. When decisions are made, then, all jurisdictions are obligated to follow the decisions of the World Conference in their policies and programs. Alternative programs may not be bad in themselves, but when they compete for the time, resources, and energies of the people, they detract from a unified movement and delay the accomplishment of the overall mission of the church.

When study materials or programs are originated in local jurisdictions, they should be in response to particular needs or opportunities in those jurisdictions. They should supplement and coordinate with the overall church courses and programs developed under the direction of the First Presidency, not replace them or compete with them. The church's unity is embodied in the willingness of the jurisdictions to develop their programs within the framework of, and consistent with, the decisions of World Conferences and the leadership of the First Presidency.

The leaders of jurisdictions are responsible for interpreting the decisions of World Conferences and the policies of the First Presidency to their jurisdictions, and for their implementation. Leaders need to remember that they are representing the World Church in their functioning. Every leadership function, including presiding over services, suggests a basic and substantial acceptance and support of World Church policies and leadership. Ministers of the church have been told in modern-day scripture that "their right to free speech, their right to liberty of conscience, does not permit them as individuals to frustrate the commands of the body in conference assembly" (D. and C. 125:16b). This principle should be understood and followed in the ministry of every member.

The unified movement of the church depends on a broadly shared understanding and acceptance of its purposes and programs. While there will always be differences in thought, as much as possible there needs to be widespread understanding of the church's overall mission and plans for its accomplishment.

After World Conferences have adjourned, persons should review the happenings and decisions of the Conference to understand the significance of the decisions for their own areas of ministry. Jurisdictional leaders and those who participated in the World Conference should be utilized as resource persons for this review.

The work of a delegate should not be regarded as finished when the Conference adjourns. Being a responsible delegate includes reporting to the jurisdiction and helping to interpret what happened at the Conference. This type of "debriefing" will assist each jurisdiction to join its efforts with others in accomplishing the overall programs and objectives of the World Church.

There is no single way to "debrief" the events of a World Conference. Each group will emphasize different segments which have the greatest significance for their own areas of responsibility and interest in the church's mission. Each debriefing, however, should include the "broad view" and a historical perspective. Current decisions need to be related to the understandings which have led to them. Only by understanding the past to some extent can current progress be measured toward long-range goals. Decisions also need to be seen from the perspective of worldwide mission if all members are to appreciate the immensity of God's love and the significance of the work to which all are called.

Certain approaches may be helpful in understanding the significant events of a World Conference:

A. Analysis of reports of the presiding quorums and of sermons and addresses of the World Church officers is a good way to begin. These typically report recent progress of the church in its mission with a world view, and the hopes and plans of the World Church leadership for the future directions for the church. Reports of task forces furnish information about specific areas of concern which have been investigated for the church. These usually include recommendations for action, not only for the World Church, but for the jurisdictions.

B. Analysis of the budget adopted will indicate the programs to receive material support from the World Church for implementation.

C. Analysis of legislation which was passed will reveal statements of policy, administrative procedures, and program directions of significance for all jurisdictions. If several items of legislation were adopted, they may be considered in groupings in a series of sessions. Legislation should be analyzed for (1) affirmations containing stated philosophies or understandings of the body, and (2) actions establishing policies or programs and relating these to the overall work of the church.

D. Analysis of proposed legislation which did not pass is also important. This may reveal significant areas of concern which may well deserve attention and activity, even if the World Conference did not adopt the legislation. Also, concerns and feelings of minorities are often reflected in unpassed resolutions. These deserve consideration and constructive response even if their viewpoints are not adopted as policy for the church.

E. Reports of "extracurricular activities" of the World Conference can be useful. These may include meetings of professional associations, gatherings of interest groups, institutional exhibits, and many others. Reports on these activities can give a panoramic view of the efforts of church members in mission and broaden the vision of opportunities for service.

F. A revelatory document, if one was presented, should be examined for the enlightenment it gives regarding the church's mission and how each should relate to it. Each member should seek for an understanding and be open to a personal confirming witness of God's Word when it is given to the church.

G. Articles in the *Saints Herald* in the months following World Conferences often contain observations and testimonies of other persons at the Conference. These can broaden the understanding and increase the appreciation of the workings of God in the church.

H. Videotape reports, produced by the Electronic Media Commission, are available for rental from the Resource Center, or by purchase from Herald House. These give viewers a sense of being at the Conference.

"Debriefing" in the jurisdictions is for a purpose much greater than just to satisfy the curiosity of persons about what happened at World Conference. It is to help all members understand the directions the World Church is taking to accomplish its mission, and the ways the jurisdiction and individual members can best take part in the overall work.

Frequently, World Conference decisions recommend (or even require) actions within the jurisdictions. Administrative and judicial policies decided in World Conference become policies for the whole church, and such review of Conference actions can help jurisdictions understand the reasons for policies which are established. When the reasons for their adoption are understood, policies are followed much better within any organization.

Resolutions passed at Conferences need to be studied for any responsibilities they place on jurisdictions. For example, a resolution in 1972 placed on all jurisdictions the responsibility to expand opportunities for women to be "represented in the administrative decision making of the church."[5] The 1978 resolution encouraging "repression of unnecessary wants" to help members "to best accomplish a saintly response to the concern for world hunger"[6] applies to every member in every jurisdiction. The 1980 legislation about "Youth Ministries Day" requests each pastoral unit to give recognition to the participation and contribution of children and youth in the jurisdictions.[7] In 1982, resolutions on "Peace" and "Nuclear Arms Reduction" were adopted by the Conference, calling for individual members and administrators to take specific actions to express the church's concerns on these subjects.[8]

Task force reports should be well studied. Reports in the past from the Task Force on Aging, the Task Force on Single Life-Style, the Committee on Ministry of the Unordained, and others have had specific recommendations for actions by jurisdictions. If task force reports are not well studied, and the recommendations in them seriously considered, jurisdictions will often miss opportunities for significant ministry.

Through all of the debriefing process, a primary question should be for each member and jurisdictional unit, "As a result of this Conference, what different understandings and actions are now required of us?" It is through implementation at the "grass roots" level that the legislative decisions of World Conference find their most important expression.

World Conferences are times when the church, after the example of Christ, should be about the Father's business, in particular and specific ways, and with unified purpose. All need to join in planning how to "labor together" best with their God-given gifts and to affirm that "neither death, nor life, nor angels, nor principalities, nor powers, nor things present, nor things to come, nor height, nor depth, nor any other creature, shall be able to separate us from the love of God, which is in Christ Jesus our Lord" (Rom. 8:38-39).

Each person needs to feel truly a part of the body. "There should be no schism in the body; but . . . members should have the same care one for another. And whether one member suffer, all the members suffer with it; or one member be honored, all the members rejoice with it" (I Cor. 12:25-26). When this type of love prevails, the church truly will be sharing the good news of Christ throughout the world.

SUMMARY

Manifesting universal principles in varied situations around the world requires a strong organic unity in the midst of pluralism. The World Conference acts for the entire church, and each area needs to understand the implications of World Conference actions for its jurisdiction. Delegates' responsibilities include reporting to their jurisdictions. Both official and extracurricular happenings at World Conferences should be systematically reviewed.

REFERENCES

1. "The Mission and Future of the Church," presented in First Presidency Meetings (January 1981), 1-2.
2. "Philosophy and Policy of Mission," Council of Twelve statement at First Presidency Meetings (January 1981).
3. Rules of Order III:16.
4. WCR 386.
5. WCR 1116.
6. WCR 1148.
7. WCR 1162.
8. WCR 1177 and 1178.

CHAPTER 17
Subordinate Jurisdictions

KEY CONCEPT: In the church there are organizational subdivisions with individual functions in their communities. These are related within larger jurisdictions to carry out the administrative and legislative functions necessary to the work of the church.

"Form follows function" is a simple statement of the best principle for developing an organization's structures. The first step in planning should be to examine the purposes for the organization's existence, and to relate everything else that is done to those purposes. The second step is to determine what functions are essential to accomplishing the organization's purposes. After these are defined it is time for the third step—determining which forms can best accomplish those functions. Forms, in this sense, include all the social and physical structures of the organization, the roles for its people, the design of its facilities, budget items, policy statements, programs, and other.

The principle, form follows function, is evident in God's instructions for the church. The organization established by divine guidance exists to serve divine purposes, not just for its own sake. Every part of the structure has functions to help serve these divine purposes. God's instructions have not fully defined all aspects of organization and functioning, but provide a framework for the church as it develops the forms which will best serve the functions necessary to accomplish its mission.

"Organizational structure is designed to make possible the orderly administration of the church and its ministries."[1] Different administrative subdivisions are needed to serve various functions in the organization. Local units (e.g., congregations and branches) exist to respond to needs and opportunities in individual communities and locales. Smaller units are grouped together into districts, stakes, and metropoles to derive strength from coordinated efforts, and for an identity and a functional relationship with the church as a whole.

Procedures established by World Conferences for the business of all subordinate jurisdictions include the following:

A. Advance notification must be given to the World Church officers having jurisdiction over the area, including the date and the nature of the business scheduled.[2]

B. Presiding over the meeting or conference is usually by the designated presiding officer of the jurisdiction (stake or district president, or other). On the request or in the absence of this officer, the presiding function may be assumed by the counselors, or (especially in an emergency) by the presidency of a higher jurisdiction, or by World Church officers (for example, First Presidency, Council of Twelve, or other minister having jurisdiction).[3]

C. Parliamentary procedure, in areas where it is familiar, is according to *Robert's Rules of Order*.[4] The basic law of the church as included in its scriptures, and in *Rules and Resolutions,* takes precedence if there is any difference with *Robert's Rules of Order.*[5] (See chapter 12.)

D. The agenda is suggested in some cases, as listed in the Rules of Order.[6] This "order of proceedings" is appropriate for most jurisdictional meetings.

The functions of conferences and business meetings of the jurisdictions of the church are, in most ways, the same as for World Conferences:

A. Sustaining and electing officers. Several jurisdictional officers are elected (particularly in branches and districts). Others are appointed by the appropriate presider and sustained in the conference or business meeting. A description of the appointive and elective offices is found in the Church Administrator's Handbook.

B. Approval of a budget. Each jurisdiction is to "follow the policy of operating on an approved financial budget."[7] Budgeting should reflect serious financial planning for accomplishing God's mission in the jurisdiction. To state goals for outreach and then spend resources internally indicates a lack of understanding of what budgeting is. A budget showing realistic provision for ministries, both for nurturing and for reaching out, demonstrates that the body is serious about God's work.

C. Receiving reports. Those who assume leadership roles have a responsibility to report periodically to the body of what has been done on its behalf. All leaders are actually accountable in two directions—to the World Church through the appropriate presiding officers at the next level, and to the jurisdictions in which they give leadership. The reporting functions in smaller jurisdictions are less formal than the reports given by presiding officers and quorums to World Conferences. Accountability of a leader to the people depends not on the formality of the report, but on the integrity with which it is given.

D. Adopting legislation.

Every such conference has authority to legislate for those it represents as long as it does not usurp rights lawfully centered elsewhere. For example, no branch can legislate for the district, such as requiring certain acts on the part of district officers; no branch or district can enact binding legislation on matters of World Church importance, such as setting up the conditions of church membership; and no field jurisdiction or World Conference can change the basic law of the church, such as the law concerning the mode of baptism.[8]

Policies may be legislated only for the jurisdiction the assembly represents, and are "subject always to the resolutions of World Conference and to the advice of the officers in matters committed to them under the law."[9]

Legislation relating to World Church affairs may be recommended by stakes, districts, or by branches in unorganized areas to the World Conference for enactment.[10] Branches may consider legislation relating to the next higher jurisdiction's affairs and recommend its enactment by that jurisdiction's conference.[11]

In brief, as long as their actions are consistent with World Church law and the policies set by higher jurisdictions, the members of any jurisdiction may make final decisions on matters which pertain to their own jurisdiction, and may recommend actions by the next higher jurisdiction. Careful consideration should be given, and processes of conferring followed, in preparing and refining recommendations to be forwarded to a higher jurisdiction. On many occasions, World Conference time has been taken up by resolutions that were carelessly written and passed without refinement by the jurisdictions that forwarded them.

E. Acting to accept revelatory statements is reserved for World Conferences—it is *not* a function of subordinate jurisdictions.[12]

Specific instruction has been given to the church for branches and districts, but is appropriate for other jurisdictions as well, that their

affairs are not to be conducted by manifestations of the Spirit unless these directions and manifestations come through the regularly authorized officers.... If my people will respect the officers whom I have called and set in the church, I will respect these officers; and if they do not, they cannot expect the riches of gifts and the blessings of direction.—D. and C. 125:14 b, c

It is understandable that persons who feel they have been given insight into God's will for the body would want to share it with others. Their insights may be entirely correct, but there are limitations on how they may be presented. God does not coerce people in decision making; those who would speak for God, therefore, should not be coercive. The use of "thus saith the Spirit..." in an assembly by a member tends to end discussion. It strongly inhibits the rights of other members to participate who may feel they have insights, too, but who would hesitate to share them if they happen to be different from the first member's statement of God's will. Therefore, manifestations of the Spirit for jurisdictions are to be given only through the proper presiding officers, who are responsible for expressing them in ways that do not coerce the body, but are respectful of its rights. Other members may have their own confirming insights, but out of respect for the rights of others must leave their presentation to the proper presiding officers.

As in World Conferences, all of the legislative functions at various levels within the church are best carried out in a nurturing fellowship and worship that helps keep God's purposes in clear focus. People who meet to do business with loving concern for one another and a desire to do the Lord's work have different priorities in legislation from those not so motivated. This marks a difference between being prophetic and being just another organization. God calls the church to a divine work; the people in turn choose to respond positively to the call.

Doing God's work starts with the desire, a devotion to God's purposes. But devotion alone does not suffice. It also takes the necessary competence to program time and resources for effective ministry, as well as the actual performance of those ministries. Competence is also needed in evaluating repeatedly how the work is progressing, and refining plans in light of new problems and opportunities.

Planning, doing, evaluating, and planning again introduces the concept of a "feedback loop," which is necessary to assess progress toward goals. An organization may state lofty goals, legislate into being wonderful-sounding programs, expend tremendous amounts of energy and resources in those programs, and have no idea how it is actually progressing—unless it provides for the necessary feedback to the legislative body. The body needs to know what has been done to implement its decisions and how successful the implementation has been. The specific system of feedback is not critical; it is just essential that some type of responsible feedback occur at every level of decision making in the body.

One way of analyzing a "feedback loop" uses the mnemonic, "soapier:"

S—Subjective statement of a problem or an opportunity.

O—Objective data available to evaluate the situation

A—Assessment of the situation in light of the data

P—Plan of action to solve the problem or take advantage of the opportunity

I—Implementation of the plan—actually doing it

E—Evaluation of the success of the plan

R—Reporting back and starting the process over again

The last three steps of the process too often are not done. They are essential, however, in a church which recognizes its accountability to God for the use of its time and resources.

Some elements necessary for responsible decision making and progression toward goals might seem to be obvious, but are often forgotten in some groups. These elements include the following:

A. Good records of decisions of the body. Records should be retained and organized for reference by the members and the guidance of the administrators. When administrators change, they may be unaware of policies which have been established by their jurisdictions unless organized records are kept.

B. Advance preparation. Proposed budgets, lists of nominees and appointments for leadership positions, proposed statements of policies, etc., should be prepared sufficiently in advance to be made available to the membership prior to the meetings where they are to be considered.

C. Consistency with policies and programs of the World Church. The church is called to be one body with many members having differing functions. Though variation in application will occur due to specific problems and opportunities in certain areas, the programs of an area should be related to the overall program objectives of the World Church.

D. Internal consistency between stated philosophies and the budgets and programs which are adopted. The way the funds are used and the time is spent, in the final analysis, tells what is *really* important to a body. With an "eye single to the glory of God" jurisdictions must examine all they do in the light of God's will, and set priorities for budgets and programs accordingly.

The eternal truths of the gospel remain constant. The forms in which those truths are expressed vary with time and location. From culture to culture, different forms will have better capabilities for expressing the same truths. The church is a community of people who share a vision of God's will and who continually strive to express more faithfully the good news of the gospel in better ways. They therefore organize according to the manner designed of God, with all the creativity and ability God has placed within them.

Seen as the body of Christ, the church's jurisdictions are its arms and legs, hands and feet, which perform many of its functions. As the hands are controlled in their functions by the brain, the jurisdictions take overall direction from World Church leadership. As hands must go through much effort and repetitive practice to make the fine movements necessary to play a piano concerto, jurisdictions must continually seek to coordinate and refine their ability to perform their functions in the work of the church.

The purpose of the church is to fulfill the commission of its Lord to go into all the world and make disciples of all nations (Matthew 28:18-19 Inspired Version). The singular purpose of the congregations and jurisdictions, the headquarters divisions and commissions, the general officers and the institutions of the church is to proclaim the good news of what God has done in Christ.... The church exists as an instrument through which Christ reveals to persons the nature of his redeeming ministry and calls them to his service. Paul's New Testament description of the church as the "body of Christ" emphasizes that the church serves the divine purpose of human salvation.... Its organizational forms and administrative procedures are designed to facilitate the witnessing, revealing, redeeming ministry of the gospel. Under the guidance of the Holy Spirit such forms and procedures respond to the changing needs of each generation.[13]

SUMMARY

The church exists as the body of Christ to serve the divine purpose of human salvation. All of its functions should be directed toward this purpose. In turn, all of its forms, including both its social and its physical structures, should be derived from the functions which are to be served. The church is one body, but with many parts. Overall policies and programs are established in World Conferences, to be administered by the proper church leaders. Subdivisions of the church (jurisdictions) exist to respond to needs and opportunities in different parts of the world. These vary in size from units in single communities, to progressively larger groupings for purposes of strength, identity, and coordination within the World Church. Legislative functions are appropriate for most types of jurisdictions, and need to be carried out with the same care for Christian ways of conferring as at the World Church level. Because conditions change over the years, forms must continually be adapted to serve the divine purpose.

REFERENCES

1. *1985 Church Administrators Handbook,* 11.
2. Rules of Order VI:43, VII:46, VIII:55.
3. Ibid., VII:47, VIII:53, IX; WCR 1097.
4. WCR 1156.
5. Robert, Henry M., *Robert's Rules of Order* (1981), 9.
6. Rules of Order VII:49, VIII:58.
7. WCR 1008.
8. Rules of Order II:12.
9. Ibid., VI:43, VII:46.
10. Ibid., V:34, VI:43; WCR 1169.
11. Ibid., VIII:52.
12. WCR 709.
13. *Church Administrators Handbook,* 11.

CHAPTER 18
Responsibilities of Individual Members and Leaders

KEY CONCEPT: All members and leaders of the body have responsibilities to participate intelligently and considerately in the business affairs of their jurisdictions and of the World Church.

The church is its people, not buildings, not sets of beliefs or forms of worship. It is not a disembodied set of propositions and principles; it is the lives of its people. Facilities and doctrines and the nature of worship are very important, but only insofar as they serve to bring people into right relationships with God and with each other.

The purpose of the church is to be a community of people in whom the love of God as shown in Christ guides their thoughts and actions. This love is seen in the specific ways that persons relate and care for others, both individually and corporately. A loving spirit is present as people share views, make policy decisions, plan programs, and work together to carry them out. In all areas of ministry, both members and leaders act intelligently and responsibly within the structure of the church's theocratic democracy.

"Movement toward the development of the kingdom is possible only through an intelligent, considering, and consenting membership. A program has no value unless those involved move freely, and in the right spirit, toward participation."[1]

All members have several characteristic responsibilities related to doing the business of the church. These are essential both for delegates to World Conferences, and for those who participate at jurisdictional levels, including committees, departments, and commissions of congregations.

A. Activity. Every member is important to the body, and the body suffers when the contribution of any member is withheld. Even if one does not participate in discussion other than as a listener, one's presence and votes are important indicators of support and make the member much more properly informed and involved in the program and progress of the church.

B. Preparation. Preparation should be by prayer and by study of the scriptures, history, and current information which has bearing on the mission of the church. The prepared member will review the minutes of previous Conferences, read the reports which have been submitted, research agenda items which are due to come up, prepare appropriate legislation in advance of the sessions, and, if appropriate, make notes to speak from if planning to enter discussion. The prepared member will take part in the hearing sessions, or if unable to attend a particular hearing will ask someone who did attend to share the salient points of the discussion.

Informed and prepared participants can move the sessions along effectively. When a Conference seems to be getting "tied up" in confusion and differences, and a delegate says just the right thing or makes a motion that brings it all together, it is because that person has prepared.

C. Respect. There is no substitute for respect by each member for the worth and rights of other members and of the body collectively.

D. Participation. Participation is essential if consensus or common consent are to be achieved. Views which are not heard cannot be considered. Conferences and business meetings need the courageous, respectful voice of each member who can add to the information of the group or to the viewpoints which should be considered.

Proper participation also includes intelligent voting. Failure to vote is itself often tantamount to making a decision. If the issues are difficult, votes need to represent the best thinking of as many persons as possible. Votes representing a limited portion of the body can get the business done, but will not have the powerful effect of a decision made with participation and widespread support throughout the entire body.

E. Initiative. Initiative and creativity are necessary among the members of a body which tries to be prophetic. Every group needs catalysts who can sense what should be done and what is the will of the body and put it into words. The body needs those with sufficient understanding to develop meaningful statements for dialogue or for adoption as legislation, and who in turn will present these statements in their jürisdictions or quorums, in the hearing committees, or on the conference floor when appropriate. Nothing ever gets done by the many that does not begin with the initiative of a few (or perhaps just one).

F. Openmindedness. Openmindedness is a necessary attribute of a member of the church. This should not eliminate strong convictions but each should recognize that no one knows everything about even a limited subject area. All minds need to be open to further light which can come from God in many ways, including discussion by another person at a World Conference, even if there is disagreement. Only by recognizing their own limited knowledge and being willing to consider honestly the viewpoints of others can persons participate with integrity in attempts to reach consensus or common consent.

G. Support. Support of the properly made decisions of World Conference and other jurisdictions is an obligation of members once those decisions have been made. There are times and places to express disagreements, including (in the appropriate meetings) attempts to change the decisions which have been made previously. Time and further light sometimes show that a decision was possibly not the best, at least for the present time. But when a decision of the body is in force, members should try to make it work, and certainly not try to frustrate the efforts of others who are trying to abide by it. It has been said that a second-best decision carried out well is far better than the best decision done poorly.[2] Many may have thought that some decisions made were not the best, but in working to carry them out found that they were good and progress was made. In its collective decisions the body may be proved to have had more wisdom than the individual who at first did not agree.

Decisions are validated as they guide actions which further the work of the church. This depends on the support of the membership to apply the decisions of the World Conference. Whereas the Conference determines policies and programs in broad ways, specific implementation depends on the creative support of leaders and members. Through creative supportive actions, members best learn the meaning of such scriptures as "All are called according to the gifts of God unto them" (Doctrine and Covenants 119:8b).

Support for the church also means support for one another as different individuals contribute their gifts to different parts of the work. This is the type of support that causes persons to take joy and give encouragement when others assume work for which they first lack either the time, the talent, or even the inclination to do. It is fortunate that not all have the same abilities and interests; for by having many talents among the members the work can go more effectively into many more places throughout the world. Individuals should look into themselves for talents which can be expressed in ministry, and know that when they serve they have the support of others working in ther own areas. Members can thus be "sent" by one another to work where they can do best, showing that the scripture, "Go ye into all the world, and whatsoever place ye can not go into, ye shall send, that the testimony may go from you into all the world, unto every creature" (Doctrine and Covenants 83:10a), pertains not only to far distant worlds, but to places nearby as well.

Support is also owed to properly designated leaders at every level, including priesthood leaders serving according to their offices and callings, and other members selected for leadership positions. Leaders can function only insofar as those who follow respect and support them. It is essential that members should respect leaders in their positions—at the same time, leaders should be deserving of respect.

Good leaders, while having individual duties related to their specific positions, share many characteristics in common, again at every jurisdictional level.

Servanthood was the model given us by Jesus. Those who would lead act as the servants of those they lead. "Let this mind be in you, which was also in Christ Jesus; who, being in the form of God, thought it not robbery to be equal with God; but made himself of no reputation, and took upon him the form of a servant, and was made in the likeness of men" (Phil. 2:5-7).

Preparation should be done by leaders with particular attention to refining leadership skills which can serve the body. These include familiarity with church laws, policies, and organization, and with parliamentary procedure as a tool to be used in facilitating the democratic process. Their preparation should include gathering and disseminating information to help the membership make sound judgments and informed decisions.

Perspective and a sense of proportion are important for leaders. This includes a good overview of the mission of the church and a specific vision for the jurisdiction and its ministries.

Communication skills are important for many reasons. Leaders need the ability to communicate to members the requirements of World Church laws, policies, and program outlines, so the jurisdictions may comply with decisions of the World Conferences. They need to be able to communicate their vision of how the jurisdiction can fulfill its mission, and be able to listen to the wisdom and ideas which can come from the "grass roots." They need the communication skills to assist members to relate to one another and to World Church programs.

Presiding skills are essential to leaders of all deliberative bodies, and need to be coupled with the understanding that authority is easy to abuse, even unintentionally and unknowingly. Those who preside need to know proper parliamentary procedure and use it effectively. They should provide the body with necessary information defining the choices available making recommendations when appropriate, but refraining from coercing the body in its decisions. They need to elicit comprehensive participation by the various members of the body, so that as many responsible viewpoints as possible may be heard before decisions are made. They need to exercise the kind of leadership that protects the rights and draws forth the participation of those members who are shy or who are not familiar with legislative processes.

Respect is due from leaders for the rights of the church as a whole and of each individual in it. Leaders should serve as facilitators of the democratic processes in helping the body achieve consensus or common consent. Respect by a leader for a jurisdiction includes accepting and implementing its properly made legislative decisions whether or not they agree with the leader's personal views.

Support for World Church policies and programs is an obligation of all leaders. They also owe support to the decisions their jurisdictions have made in implementing the program of the World Church in their areas. Support between leaders and other members is a mutual matter as all attempt to fulfill their individual roles in the work of the church. The processes of accountability to the World Church are defined in scripture, World Conference decisions, and administrative policies of the First Presidency. Accountability to jurisdictions is through presiding responsibly with respect for the rights of the body, administering according to church law and the decisions of the body, and by reporting to their jurisdictions what their actions have been as leaders in service to the body.

The scriptures emphasize the importance of all members of the body. Each member and leader should appreciate and support one another in their functioning in the body. When love and unity are sufficient so that when one member suffers all suffer, and when one member is honored all feel honored, the work will hasten. The attitude which will bring all members and leaders to this point is caught up in Doctrine and Covenants 4.

Now, behold, a marvelous work is about to come forth among the children of men, therefore, O ye that embark in the service of God, see that ye serve him with all your heart, might, mind, and strength, that ye may stand blameless before God at the last day; therefore, if ye have desires to serve God, ye are called to the work, for, behold, the field is white already to harvest, and lo, he that thrusteth in his sickle with his might, the same layeth up in store that he perish not, but bringeth salvation to his soul; and faith, hope, charity, and love, with an eye single to the glory of God, qualifies him for the work. Remember, faith, virtue, knowledge, temperance, patience, brotherly kindness, godliness, charity, humility, diligence. Ask and ye shall receive, knock and it shall be opened unto you. Amen.

SUMMARY

The church is a community consisting of unique individuals with varied talents needing to be blended together to accomplish the work of the kingdom. This blending of diverse abilities depends upon effective communication and leadership to coordinate individual efforts into a unified work. The success of the process is manifest by openmindedness, active participation, preparation, initiative, respect for others, and support for leadership. Leaders are required who will serve the body with respect for its rights and for its identity as a part of the World Church, who will develop skills in communicating and presiding to facilitate decision making by the body, and who will regularly give a proper accounting of their leadership responsibilities, both to World Church representatives and to the jurisdictions which they serve.

REFERENCES

1. *Church Members Manual,* 85.
2. Attributed to Benjamin Disraeli.

INDEX

229